CW00660219

STAGE FIGHTING

STAGE FIGHTING

A Practical Guide

Jonathan Howell

THE CROWOOD PRESS

First published in 2008 by
The Crowood Press Ltd
Ramsbury, Marlborough
Wiltshire SN8 2HR

www.crowood.com

© Jonathan Howell 2008

All rights reserved. No part of this publication may be reproduced or transmitted in any form or by any means, electronic or mechanical, including photocopy, recording, or any information storage and retrieval system, without permission in writing from the publishers.

British Library Cataloguing-in-Publication Data
A catalogue record for this book is available from the British Library.

ISBN 978 1 84797 046 6

Photographs by Graham Burke
Illustrations by Caroline Pratt

It is strongly recommended that all safety and security measures are adhered to when attempting any of the exercises in this book. The author and publisher do not accept responsibility in any manner whatsoever for any loss, damage, injury, adverse outcome or liability of any kind incurred as a result of the use of any of the information contained in this book, or reliance upon it.

Typeset by Jean Cussons Typesetting, Diss, Norfolk

Printed and bound in Singapore by Craft Print International

CONTENTS

DEDICATION

To all those who have studied and worked with me, who have challenged me, maddened me, inspired and delighted me.

This is for you.
Deep joy!

ACKNOWLEDGEMENTS

While this page appears almost at the beginning of the book, it was actually the last page I wrote, for it is not until you are almost finished that you realize just how many people have had an influence on your journey.

In order to thank them all, I would have to live this life again.

However, it will be immediately obvious to you how much thanks I owe to Tiffany Antoniuk and 'Kombat' Kate Waters for appearing with me; to Graham Burke for his sterling photography; to Erik Berg for the ballet photographs; and to Kathy West and the combat team on the 2007 NODA summer course.

What you will read in this book comes from a fund of knowledge and experience accumulated over the years in the company of many excellent teachers, many of whom I am proud to call 'friend'.

Thanks are due to Henry Marshall, who began it all; to Bill Hobbs and John Waller, who were, to me, pillars of the Society of British Fight Directors; to Michael Poynor, for my first taste of stage fighting and to B.H. Barry, who introduced me to aikido and the joys of unarmed stage combat; to Steve Wilsher, for a few dirty Welsh tricks and to Derek Ware, for his endless fund of stories and unfailing bonhomie.

I am also grateful to those who crossed oceans to come and 'play' at the Bristol Old Vic Theatre School, who are now teachers and fight directors in their own right: Andrew Fraser, Kombat Kate, Tiffany Antoniuk, Jean-Marc Perret, John Ficarra and Tim Klotz (to whom my thanks especially go, for *Cyrano*).

There are now many stunning teachers of stage combat and I can acknowledge here only a few of the groups to which they belong, and with whom I have had the privilege of working: the International Order of the Sword and the Pen and their 'Paddy Crean' workshops; the Nordic Stage Fight Society; Fight Directors Canada; the Society of American Fight Directors; the Society of Australian Fight Directors, Inc.; and the British Academy of Dramatic Combat.

Comrades-in-arms include: from Sweden, Peppe Ostensson and Maria Winton; from the USA, Brad Waller, David 'Pops' Doersch, Michelle Ladd, Eric Frederickson and David Boushey; from Canada, J.P. Fournier, Daniel Levinson, Jean-Francois Gagnon, Paddy Crean and John Brogan; from Belgium, Jacques Cappelle; from Norway, the Kippersunds and Kristoffer Jorgensen; from Denmark, Tina Robinson-Hanson and Bo Thomas; from Estonia, Teet and Tiit Kask; from South Africa, Marie-Hélène Coetzee; from Australia, Scott Witt, Kyle Rowling and Nigel Poulton; and from New Zealand, Tony Wolf.

And, finally, to my sister Jennifer and her family, Michael, David, Anthony and Kathryn, who have been fervent supporters, since for ever.

PREFACE

'Where shall we begin. There is no beginning – start where you arrive. Stop before what entices you and work. You will enter little by little into the entirety. Method will be born in proportion to your interest.'

(Auguste Rodin)

Dear Reader

First, please do not be offended at the use of the masculine pronoun, instead of the feminine. Until someone comes up with a non-gender-specific pronoun, it remains simply a tool of convenience and implies neither ability nor suitability.

Second, all the techniques are written for the right-hander. Left-handers should not force themselves to do the techniques right-handed. On the contrary, they should work with their strengths; where the instructions read 'R.', they should simply read 'L.', and vice versa. (But please note also that advanced students should be able to use both sides of their body equally well.)

You can read this book all the way through or just dip into it; highlight or underline the text, make margin notes if you want to; take from it whatever helps you the most. It is, after all, your guide, your compass, to the world of stage fighting.

As to a method of work, I recommend that you study the techniques slowly and thoroughly, working through the steps. Remember that instant results usually fade away as quickly as they came.

Finally, make sure that you understand the basic concepts, the reasoning, the logic, and, most importantly, the safety elements, stated and implied, within the training methods. They have been developed to help you get good results, make you look good, and to keep you safe while doing so.

Jonathan Howell

INTRODUCTION

When I am asked what I do for a living, I often reply, somewhat tongue in cheek, 'My job as a teacher of stage fighting is to turn men into dancers and women into warriors.'

Women sometimes approach stage fighting with apprehension, but I have found that, once they discover the 'illusion' of the techniques, and understand that they can 'dance the fight' without getting hurt and that strength is not the dominating factor, they become warrior-like. Their qualities are exemplified today by such amazing female characters as Zena, Warrior Princess, Lara Croft, Charlie's Angels and the sword-wielding Chinese heroines portrayed so excellently by Zang Zi Yi and Michelle Yeoh in such films as *Crouching Tiger*, *Hidden Dragon* and *House of Flying Daggers*.

As to the men, an ancient Swordmaster once said, 'Never put a sword into the hand of a man who can't dance.' I imagine the dancing masters of the past who taught court etiquette, as well as the Art of the Sword, would have echoed that principle, as they tried to get their charges to move more elegantly. I certainly do.

To prepare yourself for stage fighting you will need to do two things:

1. improve your general physicality; you will need to be able to move and throw yourself around with confidence, in action and reaction;
2. learn the fighting techniques.

What is meant by the term 'stage fighting? Does it imply the use of 'real' techniques, as seen perhaps in martial arts or a self-defence class, staged in a piece of choreography, with punches and kicks, sword strokes or stick strikes that are 'pulled', so that the combatants will not hurt themselves? Alternatively, does the use of the word 'stage' mean, in fact, that the fighting itself is a piece of theatrical 'magic', with all its techniques of mis-direction?

Theatre is 'magic'. Magic is an 'illusion'. Theatrical fighting is an 'illusion'.

For me, stage fighting is all about the 'grand illusion'. However, if you are to succeed in creating an illusion, you must first understand the mechanics of the reality.

There are two types of techniques:

1. those that are derived from battle, in which combat techniques – martial arts – have meant the survival of a warrior;
2. those that are born out of instinct; such techniques are spontaneous and naturally spring to a person's aid *in extremis*.

In stage fighting, the techniques are broken down into their component parts, such as 'who does what to whom', and, without changing the appearance of the attack, the energies and controls are then reversed, leading to the stage-combat concepts of 'reverse energy', 'mis-direction', 'victim control', and so forth. Stage combat also removes the usual end result of the 'real' techniques, which is pain.

Finally, the techniques are staged – placed in the 'performance' space – so that the audience gets to see what the fight director wants them to see, and misses that which he/she wishes to hide.

The aim of this book is to take you behind the scenes, to give you the actor's perspective and, un-masking the illusionist, to show you how the tricks are done. It will inform you, guide you and, step by step, take you through various unarmed and weapon techniques. Working from this book, you will be able to learn, rehearse and, ultimately, perform fights on stage, always remembering your responsibility for the safety of both your partner and yourself.

In studying anything new, most individuals tend to make better progress with a teacher than on their own, so it is worth trying to find one. Meanwhile, let this book be your guide, companion and a constant reference on your journey.

'And now, Harry, let us step out into the night and pursue that flighty temptress, adventure.'

(J.K. Rowling, *Harry Potter and The Half-Blood Prince*)

1 GENERAL PRINCIPLES

Always be positive in your attitude. Don't say, 'I can't do it'. Say, 'I can't do it yet'!

WORKING WITH A PARTNER

You can of course learn the techniques and theory in this book without a partner, but with a partner you will learn the practicalities of distance, targets, reaction timing, and much more. You will become two actors 'dancing a fight' together while the audience sit and watch two characters battling away. By the time you reach that performance, you will have learned to trust your partner to make you look good, just as your partner will have learned to rely on you to return the compliment.

> Training is different from rehearsing and performing. In training, you teach and train the body to be able to perform a number techniques. In rehearsals, you choose specific techniques that suit the character and scene, and string them together in a piece of choreography.

PRACTICALITIES

What to Wear

Wear clothing that is comfortable, and allows you to move and, almost certainly, sweat. Shoes should be sensible, with a non-slip sole and a good heel, and support your feet.

Do not wear any jewellery, including rings, watches and bangles that may scratch, earrings that may be ripped from the ear, or necklaces or chains that may strangle. Belly button decorations may make taking a blow to the stomach particularly uncomfortable.

Anything that will not come off easily should be taped firmly to the body part.

Body Contact

Body contact is difficult to avoid when fighting, especially when practising and performing unarmed combat. Many of the techniques require it and, indeed, are safer because of it. However, you do need to be sensitive to your partner's needs, fears and foibles. The whole basis of partners working together is trust, which can take a long time to develop, and can swiftly and easily be shattered.

Work it all through sensibly and responsibly, always maintaining a dialogue with your partner.

Be aware of body odour and excessive sweating. Even the most tolerant of partners will not be as willing to practise up-close-and-personal techniques if your T-shirt is soaked in sweat, if you smell bad through lack of deodorant, if you do not have clean gear. Always take with you a deodorant and an extra T-shirt or two to change into.

WARM-UPS AND WARM-DOWNS

These tend to vary according to the time

available, the mood of the group, and so on. Sometimes the company makes it compulsory, sometimes the actors are left to their own devices. Ultimately, however, it will always be a matter of self-discipline. If an actor has dialogue, he or she will always do a vocal warm-up, and the body surely deserves the same consideration.

Actors of advanced years tend to warm up more slowly and for a longer time. They either need more time to get the blood flowing and the joints mobilized or perhaps their experience makes them more crafty. However, sitting on a radiator with a cup of tea in one hand and *The Times* crossword in the other does not constitute the ideal mental or physical warm-up.

Preparation, both physical and mental, for training, is essential. It should include exercises that increase the heart rate and thereby the blood flow to the muscles, and stretching exercises to prepare the joints and muscles for the rough and tumble ahead. It should also put the individual in the right frame of mind for the work to come.

Warm-Up

The following set of warm-up exercises come from my training with the Nordic Stage Fight Society in Stange/Hamar, Norway, under the guidance of the Kippersunds, a family of wonderful Viking-warrior performers.

Start each exercise 'at attention', in the Chairman Mao position, standing straight, feet together, arms at your side.

Each exercise is made up of 2 sets of 16 counts. Set 1 is 8 counts (4 to the L. and 4 to the R.), repeated to make 16 counts in total. Set 2 is made up of another 16 counts.

The movements in the second set can be an exact repeat of the first set, but you may also develop them. The choice to maintain or develop the exercise is entirely yours.

Marching
Assume the marching position. Start with the L. foot up, then march in place 3 times, lifting the knee and opposite arm with vigour. Hold the 4th count, in position (*see* Fig 1). 32 counts in total.

Pull and Push
Set 1: stand to 'attention'. On count 'and', prepare by reaching up as you step out to the L. (*see* Fig 2, left).
Counts 1, 2: pull down × 2 (or chin a bar) as you bend your knees (*see* Fig 2, right).
Count 3: push out (as if opening doors), deepening your knee bend (*see* Fig 3, left).
Count 4: return to 'attention'.
Counts 5, 6, 7: step out to your R., 'pull × 2', then 'push'.
Count 8: return to centre.
Repeat all 8 counts.

Fig 1

Fig 2

Fig 3

Set 2: add two short out breaths on the 'pull-downs', then one longer exhalation on the 'push out'.

Punches

Use a karate-style punch, with shoulders held back (*see* Fig 4, right).

Set 1: stand to 'attention'. On count 'and', prepare by stepping out to your L. in a good lunge, R. fist on your hip.

Counts 1, 2, 3: punch R., L., R.

Fig 4

Fig 5

Fig 6

Count 4: return to face front (*see* Fig 5, right), with knees bent, fists 'cocked' at the hip.

Counts 5, 6, 7: step out to your R. in a good lunge, punching L., R., L.

Count 8: return to centre.

Repeat all 8 counts.

Set 2: try a Chinese-style or extended punch (*see* Fig 4, left).

Butterflies

Open the chest by stretching the arms, from crossed to open wide.

Set 1: stand to 'attention'. On count 'and', cross your arms at chest height, palms down.

Count 1: lunge forwards with the L. foot to a 45-degree angle, opening your arms wide (*see* Fig 6, left). On count 'and', cross the arms again, almost straightening the front knee (*see* Fig 6, right).

Count 2: lunge again, opening the arms wide.

Fig 7

Fig 8

Fig 9

Count 3: bring the feet together, facing front, and swing the arms forwards, in a circle (*see* Fig 7, left).

Count 4: bend the knees and touch the floor, or your knees (*see* Fig 8).

On count 'and', stand and cross your arms at chest height, palms down.

Counts 5, 6, 7, 8: repeat the moves, going to the R.

Repeat all 8 counts.

Set 2: repeat, this time with palms up, and, as you swing the arms, add a jump up in the air (*see* Fig 7, right).

Kicks

Set 1: stand to 'attention'.

Count 1: step back on the R. foot into the preparation position, arms up in the Fwd. High 45 degrees (*see* Fig 9).

Count 2: lifting the knee and bringing your arms to your hips, tightening the stomach at the same time, make a front snap-kick, as high as is comfortable (foot relaxed) (*see* Fig 10, right).

Count 3: return to the preparation position.

Fig 10

Fig 11

Fig 12

Fig 13

Count 4: return to standing at 'attention'.
Counts 5, 6, 7, 8: start with the L. leg.
Repeat all 8 counts.
Set 2: carry out the same preparation, but this time the kick is not snapped from the knee but 'swung' from the hip with a flexed foot, arms swinging back at the same time (*see* Fig 11).

Windmills
Set 1: stand to 'attention' (*see* Fig 12, left).
Count 1: step out to the L., raising your arms (*see* Fig 12, right).
Count 2: reach down with your R. arm to touch your L. foot (*see* Fig 13, left).
Count 3: twist your top half to face back with arms stretched high and wide (*see* Fig 13, right). Add a loud vocal breath out – 'Aaaah' – on this stretch back.
Count 4: return to 'attention'.

Fig 14

Fig 15

Count 5: start to the R., stretching out before touching your R. foot with your L. hand, and so on.

Repeat all 8 counts.

Set 2: double the toe-touches; step out on Count 1. On 'and', touch the L. foot and on Count 2, touch the R. foot. Continue with the stretch up and back on 3, and return to 'attention' on 4.

Swan Side Stretches

Set 1: stand to 'attention'.

Count 1: take a small pace out to the L., arms in a 'dancer's' stretch (stretching the lower arm in the opposite direction at the same time) (*see* Fig 14, left). On 'and', recover a little.

Count 2: stretch a little further. On 'and', recover a little.

Count 3: stretch even further. On 'and', bring the feet together, knees bent, hands stretched forwards.

Count 4: pull the hands back to the hips, as you thrust the hips forwards. Add a vocal gut-based 'hah' (*see* Fig 14, right).

Fig 16

Fig 17

Count 5: repeat to the R., and so on.
Repeat all 8 counts.
Set 2: double and syncopate the first three 'hahs', finishing with one big one.

'Singing' Toe Touches
Set 1: stand to 'attention'.
Count 1: join the hands together, palm on palm; twist them palms up and stretch to the ceiling (*see* Fig 15, left).
Count 2: touch the ground in front of your toes (or as low as you can get).

Count 3: step back on the R. leg (reverse lunge), opening the arms wide (*see* Fig 16). If you had music, this is the moment for a sung 'Aaah', following 'doh - me - so - me' in Set 1, 'so - ti - doh - so'.
Count 4: return to 'attention'.
Counts 5, 6, 7, 8: repeat with the L. foot.
Repeat all 8 counts.
Set 2: repeat all four singing stretches.

'Jumping Jacks'
Set 1: stand to 'attention'.

Count 1: jump astride, arms out wide (*see* Fig 17, left).

Count 2: jump together, and clap hands overhead (*see* Fig 17, right).

Count 3: jump astride again.

Count 4: jump back to 'attention'.

Repeat the above.

Set 2: do four 'star jumps', in the same position, but in the air, one jump taking 2 counts.

Running Steps

Start as for the first exercise, one knee and opposite arm up in the air.

Counts 1, 2, 3 are now exaggerated 'running' steps.

Count 4: hop.

Do the first 16 counts 'straight'. For the next 16 counts, turn on the spot or travel; you could try not hopping the fourth count but freezing in some extraordinary position to test your balance. Have fun with it!

Head and Neck Exercises

After all these exercises, the only part of the body not warmed up is the neck. It is vital to prepare neck and top-shoulder muscles and joints, particularly if you are going to rehearse rolls or head reactions to slaps or punches.

To warm up the head and neck, start with up-and-down exercises (×4): stand in a neutral position, looking front and centre. On Count 1, drop your chin on to your chest; Count 2, lift your head to the centre; Count 3, lift to look at the ceiling; Count 4, return to centre.

Side-to-side (×4): on Count 1, look as far L. as possible; on Count 2, return to centre; Count 3, look as far R. as possible; Count 4, return to centre.

Ear-to-ear (×4): keeping the head straight, on Count 1, drop your L. ear to your L. shoulder; Count 2, return to centre; Count 3, drop your R. ear to your R. shoulder; Count 4, return to centre. You can increase the effect by stretching down the opposite arm.

Head roll to the front: look side L., drop your chin on to your chest, roll down across and then up to look to your R. Now roll back again to the L. Repeat. You can add to the rhythm by bending your knees as you swing 'down' and straightening them on the 'up'.

Head roll to the back: look side L., let your head go back, supporting it by clenching the buttock muscles (this automatically tightens the trapezius muscle which runs up the back and into the shoulders and neck), and look across the ceiling until you arrive looking side R.

Having completed your warm-up you can now proceed to training, practice, rehearsal or performance. If you are going to performance, your next move after the warm-up should be to the 'Fight Call' (*see* page 177).

Warm-Down

While it may be common practice after a show to make your way immediately to the bar, after training and practice you should take a few minutes to 'cool', or warm down. It will help your body return to its normal routine and allow the blood to return from the working muscles to the general circulation.

Use exercises with less intensity and stretches that are held for longer. The warm-down can help reduce the chance of muscles cramping later on, and prevent stiffness, soreness or fatigue in the muscles the next day.

PRINCIPLES OF SAFETY

There will some pain in your training, from the discipline of constant repetition – as someone once said, 'While pain isn't good, getting good at something often involves pain' – but no one should ever be hurt by their partner while stage fighting. It is so easy to do stage fighting badly, and bad stage fighting can easily become dangerous. The danger may be present because the techniques have been badly taught or sloppily learned, or perhaps because some actions seem so 'natural' that they are not considered to be 'stage fighting' and so are not rehearsed.

Always rehearse beforehand the physical actions you are going to perform and always perform what you have rehearsed! There is no place for improvisation in combat performance.

In real-life fighting, an attack is generally instigated by one individual. It is the attacker's energy that drives the action, the attacker is in control, and it follows that the victim is the one who gets hurt. In stage fighting, the actors enter the world of violence, like Alice, 'through the looking glass', and find that the opposite will generally apply. The safest situation usually proves to be that in which the 'victim' of the 'attack' is actually leading the techniques and controlling the outcome.

The safety of all participants fundamentally lies in correct training and then in the correct application of that training. It is important to have faith that these techniques will keep you and your partner safe while, at the same time, helping you both 'look good'.

My Mantra

Inwardly digest and breathe the following mantra as you learn, rehearse and perform the stage-fighting techniques in this book:

Eye contact – Preparation – Action – (Sound) – Reaction.
(Sound is essential, in order to 'sell' the illusion of contact; *see* page 27, 'General Concepts' for more on this.)

Eye Contact
Before you do anything, look in your partner's eyes to check not only that the 'lights are on', but also that 'someone is at home'. If a person is not concentrating, not focused, or has 'blanked' (forgotten the next line or the next move), it will show in their eyes.

Making eye contact also gives a visual cue to your partner that you are about to do something, for example, launch an attack. A good general safety rule is: 'No eye contact, no fight!'. There are exceptions, of course, but even an unsighted attack will require a cue of some kind, such as a sound.

Preparation
This might be a physical action, for example, a winding-up; made in the opposite direction to your attack. Make sure your partner can see it – do not prepare behind your back or too low – and let the audience see it as well. They also need to 'prepare', for part of their enjoyment lies in the anticipation of what is about to happen.

Timing is important: as the attacker prepares for the attack, at the same time the victim prepares to react.

Action
This means the execution of the technique in a safe yet dramatically convincing manner.

Reaction
Your face is your link to the audience as well as to your partner. Try to keep it up so that your reactions are visible and any dialogue is audible.

The basic reaction is led by that part of the victim's body which is 'hit'. It should follow the line of the attack, and it should equal the energy of the attack (unless a 'comic' or 'heroic' reaction is intended).

The victim can then enhance the reaction by adding further body motion, such as a fall, a roll, or a flying twist or two.

GENERAL CONCEPTS OF UNARMED COMBAT

Although you may learn and practise techniques in isolation, they will eventually be performed as part of a greater entity – the *fight* – which itself is part of a greater thing – the *story*.

There are a number of general concepts that are part of the illusion that is stage fighting.

Air

When a punch/kick misses the victim, the space between the fist/foot and the victim's body is the 'air'. Angles of attack and staging will help hide this from the audience to maintain the illusion of 'contact'.

To create the illusion of contact, it has become popular (convenient) in the theatre to stage these techniques on an Upstage (U.S.) Downstage (D.S.) line (*see* page 28, 'Staging'). However, when you watch screen fights, you can generally see the face of one of the actors. Be creative, think more from the camera's point of view (P.O.V.), and consider the diagonals.

Depending on where the audience sits, their P.O.V. can change the effective line of an attack. If they are above the actors, you need to keep your attacks low; if they are below them, the attacks need to cross the target on a higher line. It is very useful to have a 'third eye' out front, to spot these things for you in rehearsal.

Balance

Balance is critical: an actor off balance is a danger to himself as well as to others around him, including the audience. This does not mean that he has to stand still. In his book *Tao of Jeet Kune Do*, Bruce Lee says that, 'Balance is the control of one's center of gravity...and might mean being able to throw one's centre of gravity beyond the base of support, chase it, and never let it get away.'

Body Lines

If you divide your body into two – one line running horizontally across the waist line – everything above the waist is in the 'high' line and everything below is in the 'low' line (*see* Appendix Diagram 1).

The front or 'inside' of your body contains your soft tissues; the back of your body, where you would wear your shell if you were a Ninja Turtle, is the 'hard' side, referred to as the 'outside'.

Choices are Good

In preparing yourself generally, train beyond the limit of your expectations. If you know that, as part of the action in a scene, you have to perform a forward roll and you have only just learnt how to do one, in performance, during the preceding scene, your focus and thoughts will be on the roll to come. If, however, you have trained yourself to do somersaults in the air, a simple forward roll will not worry you at all. You will do it as naturally and easily as the preceding dialogue.

The more physical choices you have, the more you have to offer the director and the more colour, variety and depth you can bring to your character.

Contact Technique

Contact should be light and 'pulled', and made only on to major muscle groups of the body such as the stomach, the inside of the thigh, or the back.

For students or young actors, a lot of the fun in unarmed combat is in the giving and taking of 'contact' punches and kicks, and so on. However, there are times when it is not possible. The physique of some people is not suited to taking contact, and many actors, as they grow older and possibly wiser, really do not want either to hit or be hit. There should be enough techniques in the 'physical armoury' to be able to offer alternatives that will still be as dramatically effective.

Core Strength

It is absolutely essential to maintain a strong centre to support you in everything you do.

Damage

Attacker: is your character's adrenaline pumping so much that an injury will not stop you 'till the fight is over and done'?

Victim: consider the effect of one strike, or the cumulative effect of more than one. What will ache, hurt, or cause restricted movement that you can take into the following scene?

Dialogue

You can act a fight without any dialogue at all. However, dialogue can support a fight, help drive it along, colour it and conclude it.

Some of the best dialogue moments in film fights come right in the middle of the fight, with a close-up of the hero, heroine or villain making some swashbuckling remark: 'I needed that scratch to awaken me!' says Zorro fiercely, in the 1940 film *The Mark of Zorro*; 'You've come to Nottingham once too often', declares consummate villain Basil Rathbone in the 1938 film *The Adventures of Robin Hood*.

A wordless moment of delight, equal to any dialogue, is provided by the kisses that Alejandro (Antonio Banderas) snatches from Elena (Catherine Zeta-Jones) during their sword confrontation in the stables, in the 1998 film *The Mark of Zorro*.

Distance

Distance gives you time; the greater the distance between you, the more time the victim has to see what is coming, to decide what to do, to react.

Being so close as to appear 'real', may excite you, the attacker, but it is neither exciting for an audience nor does it look any better. It is also scary for your partner.

Fighting close may be good for the camera, but in theatre you need to 'open out' the fight, particularly when fighting with weapons. Always check your 'fighting distance' with your partner, certainly visually, but also physically, for example, in unarmed combat, with an outstretched arm.

For non-contact techniques, the attacker must be either out of distance and on target (the place where 'you reach out and cannot touch someone'), or in distance but off target (close enough to touch your partner but away past the target).

To make contact, your partner must be in distance.

Safety note: the harder and/or faster the attacker wants to hit the victim, the further away the actors should be from each other. Heightened emotion will drive them closer.

Experimenting, Playing, Freestyling

Sometimes, the way to find out how the characters get what they are after (Stanislavsky) is through action (Meyerhold). You need to take it 'off the page' and 'put it on the floor'. But beware: you are not two kids in a playground "aving a go". Be heedful. Stay focused. With every new partner, every new time, start together slowly – no speed, no strength – and explore this physical jungle very carefully; it will be fun, and probably productive as well.

Having found some moves that work for the scene, make sure that you can repeat them exactly and safely, as you bring them up to a good rehearsal tempo (*see* page 28, 'Speed').

Final Picture

Do not be in a hurry. Take time. When you finish, hold it for a second. The audience will 'take a mental photograph' and retain that final image.

The camera continues to roll even after the director says 'Cut'.

Flight Path

This term may be used to denote the spatial pattern of movement. This can be as simple as the direction of a swinging punch, the pathway of its energy. However, it can also be used to denote the floor pattern created by the fighters moving around the stage. For more on this, *see* page 168.

Focus

You focus the attention of the audience. Eye contact with your partner during a fight keeps the attention of the audience fixed upon the two of you. By focusing on a block or parry, you make the audience focus on that particular moment too. This enables you to make a comment with your reaction, to lead the observer into believing that it caught you by surprise, or that you made the parry just in time, or perhaps that it was stronger than you expected.

By clapping your hand to a hurt or wounded body part, you focus the audience's attention on the injury. If you are wearing a 'blood bag' inside your shirt, you clap a hand to the 'wound' to break the bag, causing the blood to spurt out (*see* the final duel in *The Sons of the Musketeers*).

One helpful hint is to make a 'physical' reference in the following scene back to the injury – a moment's pain, twinge or stiffness. This will also contribute to excellent character development.

Forehand and Backhand

These terms relate to the side from which a blow is delivered. A right-handed person (R.) delivers a forehand strike from his R. side; a backhand from his left (L.). I prefer this way of describing a blow, particularly when having to write it down; *see* page 171, on 'Notating the Fight'.

Giving Grace

This term is most often applied to sword-fighting, however the essence is applicable to any 'strike and block', in any discipline.

What really happens in fighting?

1. The attacker's intention is to drive his attack home in on to the victim's body.
2. The victim tries to prevent the attack reaching its target by 'parrying' the strike.
3. There is a clash of energies caused by this 'obstruction of intent' and, if the attack is really parried 'hard', it will be knocked aside with force.

The action of 'giving grace' attempts to remove much of this 'forceful clash'. As the energies meet, the victim parries with the illusion of force and the attacker allows the parry to be 'successful', swinging the extended thrust smoothly away. (*See* 'Polishing the Table', page 26.)

Key to Success

'Practice is the Marrow and Quintessence of the Art...ensure that Passion, Fury nor Choler, which are the absolute Enemies to skill, in no case prevail, if you do, 'twill destroy your Judgement...'

(Zachery Wylde, *The English Master of Defence*, 1711) (Online: Kronos)

Knap

The term 'knap' is the theatrical equivalent of the sound of the attacker's body part making contact with the victim's body part – for example, a punching fist striking a face.

It can be made by different people:

Figs 18, 19, 20 *The actor prepares for a clap-knap by keeping her elbows in to the side of her body. Her R. hand claps down on to her L., as if smashing an egg. As her R. hand falls free, her L. rises to the 'struck' area; although this is a cliché, it reinforces in the mind of the audience what has just been 'struck'.*

* the attacker = striking self;
* the victim = striking self;
* shared = a strike shared between the attacker and the victim;
* a third party = another person on stage near the action; stage management in the wings;
* a recorded 'sound effect'.

The knap can be made in several different ways:

1. clap-knap: the act of clapping or, rather, slapping hands (not applauding). The fingers of one hand strike the palm of the other. The hands may be prepared either way up (see Figs 18, 19 and 20);
2. slip-hand knap: one hand is extended, perhaps holding the victim. It is then pulled back as the punching hand goes forwards and, as they pass, the fingers of the returning hand slap against the palm of the punching hand (see Fig 47, page 42);
3. shared knap: the attacker makes contact with the victim's hands or body.
4. body knap: your hand is slapped on to a muscled part of your own body, such as the stomach, thigh, chest or buttock;
5. knap on the floor: you hit a wall, a piece of furniture, and so on;
6. something is broken, such as a piece of wood; a plastic bottle is twisted; bubble wrap is crushed;
7. a sound effect may be recorded or created live on an instrument such as a synthesizer.

Where possible, the sound should approximate to the real one; for example, the sound of two hands clapping is nearer to that of a real slap than a single hand slapping the chest. However, it is worth remembering that theatrical fighting effects need to be loud, as audiences have now become conditioned to the highly exaggerated sounds created for action films, particularly the Hong Kong-style martial arts movies.

Letting Go or Releasing the Grip

If the victim is to have full control over his own energy, the attacker must never actually throw, pull or push. At some time during the execution of the technique, the attacker must release his partner and let him take over the action. This should not, however, be obvious to the audience. The attacker will still have to maintain the illusion of the attack by continuing his movement in the direction of the flow of energy, but without force – 'empty' of strength (see page 29, 'T'ai Chi').

'Hitting the Parrot'

It is easy, in the heat of the action, to misdirect attacks, seeing opposite you, not your partner, but an adversary. You can use the image of 'hitting the parrot', or the 'parrot punch', to help you in your targeting. Picture a parrot sitting on your partner's shoulder (whether you are playing a Pirate character or not). When punching, aim for that parrot and you will accurately place the punch.

'Polishing the Table'

This action follows on from 'giving grace' (see page 24). Imagine standing close to a table, your hand by your hip, holding, in this example, a cloth. Push the cloth straight forwards and then, having fully extended your arm, 'polish' out in a semi-circle returning to your hip. (Think of 'The Kid' in the The Karate Kid films – 'wax on, wax off'.)

This image relates to the semi-circular horizontal action of the attacking arm, armed or unarmed, when parried sideways. It is a particularly effective image to hold in mind when, for example, executing a series of thrusting attacks such as piston thrusts (see page 117, 'Sword Techniques'); it can, of course, be applied equally to any single technique, for example, a lunge.

Practice

The body has its own movement memory, and continual re-enforcement creates a physical pattern to which the body will 'automatically' return.

The actor must have time to practise the techniques, first singly, then as part of the fight and, finally, within the whole framework of the scene/play. As a result, in performance, the actor can rely on his body to do its own work, leaving him free to concentrate on the story-telling.

Reactions

Reactions are usually performed by the defender, although it can enhance the story dramatically if the attacker reacts as well; for example, a punch that knocks over the victim may break the attacker's hand, or the action of punching may cause the attacker to lose his balance and fall over as well.

'Real' Violence

To quote Jenn Zuko Boughn, from her book *Stage Combat: Fisticuffs, Stunts and Swordplay for Theater and Film*, 'There is no justification for 'real' violence on the stage...if done properly it loses none of its realism for the audience.'

A tactful reply to a director's suggestion that you 'just do it' is, 'Please show me how.' Get the director to slap or be slapped by the other actor; jump off that platform into three soldiers' arms; dive through that window; fall off a balcony backwards with a duvet over his head. They will soon tell you to fake it or – you can but hope – get someone in who knows not only how to do it, but also how to teach it safely, and with theatrical effect.

You should not be afraid to say 'No' if you are asked to do anything physical with which you are not comfortable. You have to live with your body for the rest of your life, so you have the right to avoid damaging it needlessly.

Reverse Energy (R.E.)

The concept of reverse energy is at the very heart of the illusion of stage combat. For example, in a 'real' strangle, the attacker's energy is in and on; in theatre, reversing the energy means it comes out and away. Whereas in reality the victim will push away, reversing the energy means holding in and on.

Both energies become equally matched, creating a 'tension'. Most importantly, should anything go wrong and the need arise to break from the grip, the victim merely releases his grip and the attacker's hands will fly out and away from his throat. Safe again.

Rhythm

Bruce Lee in his book *Tao of Jeet Kune Do* describes rhythm succinctly: 'The movements of attacking and defending work almost in rhythm with each other. They have a sequential relationship which makes the proper timing of each movement dependant on the previous movement'.

For the actors: 1, 2, 3 is 'Ready, Steady, Go' or 'Eye contact, Preparation, Action/Reaction'.

For the audience: 1, 2, 3 is 'See the Preparation, Hear the Knap, See the Reaction.'

Sound

Sound can be used to focus the attention of an audience. It can direct, mis-direct, cause pain, interest, raise the heart rate, excite, soothe or stimulate. Sound can even have the completely opposite effect, turning off the audience.

The Fighting Sound

If the sound of the knap is sharp enough, it will cause the audience to blink and miss the vital moment in the technique, when the strike does not make physical contact. They will only remember seeing the preparation and the reaction.

Vocal Sound

In theatre, vocals can be most effective, but it is not enough to rely solely on an instinctual vocal reaction. The sounds should be varied creatively, in terms of tone and pitch, as in making music.

The attacker should focus his breath on a strike, increasing its effectiveness, as every martial art teaches.

The victim can be vocally creative, remembering that some blows to the face hurt – 'Ow!' – while some to the body drive out breath, causing an 'Ooof!' Unlike the modern tennis players, however, it is not necessary to accompany every blow or reaction with a vocal grunt.

How loud should the sounds be? Some say, 'Play to the deaf man and his dog sitting in the back row.' Well, all right, let's call him 'aurally challenged'. However, some theatres are intimate spaces, while some seem to be the size of a football stadium.

Soundtrack

Without a partner it can sometimes be helpful to create a 'soundtrack' to establish and maintain rhythms in a fight. However, try to avoid 'singing along' when you perform, particularly when there is a microphone close by!

For film and TV fights, it is not necessary to make knaps at all during unarmed combat or indeed to worry about the quality of the 'swish and ting' of the swords. These will all be added on afterwards.

The sounds of combat are only a small part of the total 'soundscape' (*see* page 170).

Speed

Never think in terms of 'speed'; avoid rapid or hurried movements. Speed can make you overtake your partner, parry an attack before it happens, or attack before your partner has finished reacting to the last technique.

Think instead in terms of rhythm and pace, which can be increased or decreased; it can be taken at a slow pace, in slow motion (*see* page 29, 'T'ai Chi'); at a medium pace, or 'rehearsal speed'; or at a fast pace, or 'performance speed'.

Staging

Everyone should be aware of the staging terms used on the proscenium arch stage (*see* Appendix Diagram 2), from the actor's point of view, and on other types of stage (*see* Appendix Diagram 3).

Stillness

Fights do not have to be a constant whirl of movement. In a battle, when everyone is moving around you, it is stillness that will take the focus. In a one-on-one situation, it is movement that will generally take the focus. The attacker 'punches' and then holds still while the victim reacts; the attacker's stillness releases the audience's attention to switch focus back to the victim – and so on throughout the fight.

> When rehearsing, one of the traps to avoid is vocalizing the knaps and the sword 'swishes', for example, making *Star Wars*-style sound effects. I was demonstrating a cavalry sword drill to an actor about to shoot a scene for a television documentary on Thomas Hardy, when the sound chap spoke up, saying that he could hear some strange swishing sounds. 'Is that the sword?', he asked. Oops! I was, quite unconsciously, 'swishing along' as I swung the sword to and fro.

T'ai Chi

This is not the martial and/or meditative art in this context, but a deliberate quality of movement within a stretched time frame, as if you were doing an action in slow motion or under water, with internal energy but without external force.

The expression is used most commonly to denote the speed of a run-through or rehearsal. When 'T'ai Chi-ing' the fight, it is important that the moves are performed to their full physical limits, without, however, the speed that is required for performance.

It can also refer to fighting techniques, such as the action of a push or a pull – the arms of the attacker 'T'ai Chi-ing', or following through, after the victim, as if he had indeed used force to execute the push or pull.

The 'Value' of Action

The amount of 'Pow! Smack! Chudd!' (energy, strength, power) that you put into your attacks and, by extension, your reactions, has a value.

A simple scale of 1 to 10, as for earthquakes or wind, makes for a good indication. For example, with a slap, the 1 of a child may ineffectually swat a fly, while his 10 may make a man react with an 'Ow!' The 1 of a man would rock a child, while his 10 might easily knock another man over. It would, however, but make a giant no more than blink (*see* the film *Princess Bride*, in which the hero battles with André the Giant).

The value of an attack is relative and will, of course, depend on the 'whys and wherefores'.

Whys and Wherefores

These are the causes and effects that have a bearing upon the character and will inform the choice of the actual techniques when creating mayhem and violence. They include the character's sex, age, physical make-up, experience, motivation, emotional commitment, and needs, and so forth and so on.

2 UNARMED COMBAT

'On Foot the frowning Warriors light,
And with their pond'rous Fists renew the Fight;
Blow answers Blow, their Cheeks are smear'd with Blood,
'Till down they fall, and grappling roll in the Mud.'

(John Gay, in *Trivia*, c. 1711)

SLAPS

The basic slap seems such a simple technique to perform and yet is one of the most difficult to stage dramatically and effectively. Too often, a director will be heard to say, 'Just hit him. Everyone knows how to slap.' Indeed, some actors even ask to be hit rather than 'faking' it, because it helps them with their emotional flow. However, it is vital to learn how to fake a slap. While it is generally accepted that a woman will not slap as hard as a man and so can be persuaded to 'have a go', it is quite obvious that Othello, for example, cannot deliver a full-on contact slap to his wife Desdemona, who is usually played by a smaller and more delicate actress.

According to Jenn Zuko Boughn, in her book *Stage Combat*, 'An actor who can't act a fake slap (if taught the proper technique)

should perhaps reconsider his commitment to the scene.' I heartily agree with her, and aim to show you how simple it is to slap effectively without having to make contact. There will also be advice on how to deal with a 'contact slap'.

A slap is a strike that is delivered with the flat of something. With the hand, the target is usually the face, although it could just as easily be the back of the head, as in a clip round the ear, or, continuing with the school theme in such plays as *Daisy Pulls It Off* or *40 Years On*, a blow to the back of the thigh or a 'thwack' on the backside. However, a 'slap' could just as easily be made with a plate, a tray, a cushion or, when sword-fighting, the flat of a blade.

I was in Siena one year for the Palio, exploring the outer streets of the medieval town, when an Italian girl in her late teens ran past me towards the town gates. She was obviously upset. Before she could reach the gates, a young man raced by and caught up with her. There was a brief argument and then she slapped him hard. Without a moment's thought, he slapped her right back. The sound echoed towards me, and the street held its collective breath until they fell into each other's arms crying and kissing and laughing. Life carried on and so did I. Perhaps, I mused, in Italy the slap is an everyday occurrence.

(Opposite) A young warrior's first 'trial by combat'.

General Notes

Swinging anything close in front of someone's face is pretty scary at first, so you must give your partner time to get used to it.

Fig 21

Fig 22

There are a number of different things to consider when learning to slap:

* Out of distance: this allows a swinging arm to pass freely through the space.
* In distance: the attacker and victim are close enough to make a contact.
* Staging: to hide the 'air' between you, and the knap, from the audience.
* Attacker's stance: stand with the opposite foot to your slapping arm forward; this will help your balance and act as a brake to stop you moving forwards.
* Victim's stance: stand easily, so as to allow your body to turn when reacting.
* Cliché reaction: in reacting to a slap, some people teach the victim to bring a hand up, through the knap, to their 'smarting' cheek. This does happen in real life, sometimes, but, just as often, the victim is too shocked to move at all. Practise both and revel in the joy of choice!

Safety note: attacker – do not 'reach' for your partner as you slap; victim – you can control the distance by backing away if your partner is too close, or ask them to back off.

Techniques

Swinging Slap
This is simply a big swing of the attacker's arm across the victim, from one side to the other, out of distance. It may be done either on the forehand or the backhand.

For the *Forehand*, the attacker should prepare by pulling the slapping arm out to the side, not behind him, with a small step out sideways (*see* Fig 21). The victim must make sure she can see the slapping hand, and ready her hands to make the knap and prepare her body to react.

Action: the attacker plants his feet firmly on the ground, opens his shoulders and swings the slapping hand, with the arm straight or slightly bent, horizontally through the space between the two partners, at a height level with the other's cheek (*see* Fig 22).

The knap is a victim clap-knap.

In reaction, the victim turns her face sharply, following the hand with her eyes; as this is a hard slap, the shoulders and body should be allowed to follow on.

The *Backhand* swinging slap is generally a stronger, more 'vicious', calculated and punishing of slaps. It can be done horizontally, like the forehand slap, or on the diagonal.

As the attacker prepares for the diagonal backhand (high to low, out of distance), the victim prepares her hands for the knap (*see* Fig 23). Action: as the attacker's 'striking' hand passes, out of distance, through the target line, the victim's cheek, she knaps (*see* Fig 24). The downward angle of the blow is matched by the victim's head reaction; bending her knees will reinforce the impression of a 'forceful' slap.

Fig 23

Fig 25

Fig 24

Fig 26

For the alternative diagonal backhand (low to high, in distance), the attacker prepares from the hip. The victim is preparing for a shared knap by placing her L. hand as a target (*see* Fig 25). Action: the attacker's relaxed hand strikes the victim's, on the upward diagonal (*see* Fig 26).

Note: if you rehearse this over and over again, it will 'sting', so it is a good idea to wear light leather gloves.

In her reaction, the victim's face and body follows the diagonal path of the slap.

Sweeping or 'Windscreen-Wiper' Slap

This slap is done with a bent arm, from the elbow.

To gauge the distance, imagine there is a windscreen between you, which your hand does not cross. In preparation 'cock' the arm up, out sideways.

Action: swing through like a windscreen wiper, using the elbow as the fulcrum (*see* Fig 27). The sound is a victim clap-knap.

While the sweeping slap is a less forceful blow than the swing-through, it would still 'rock' the face of the victim. In reaction, the victim could try just turning her head, as if to say 'No!' to a person beside her, and then turn straight back to her partner.

'Pulled' Slaps

For the 'pulled-back' slap, the attacker prepares by 'cocking' the arm up and out.

Action: sweep the hand in to a point in line with the cheek, just above the victim's shoulder (*see* Fig 28); lift the hand from the elbow (*see* Fig 29); and pull it back to just above your own opposite shoulder (*see* Fig 30).

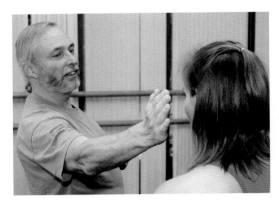

Fig 28

Fig 27

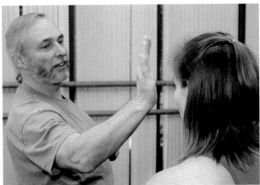

Fig 29

Fig 30

Fig 32

Reaction: as the pull-back begins, at the moment of 'hit', the victim clap-knaps and turns her head sharply to the R.

When considering staging, it is worth noting that this is one of the few slaps that can work well with the actors sideways on to the audience.

For the 'pulled up and over' slap, or clip, the target is the back of the head. In the action, the attacker's hand swings in to within an inch of the back of the head (*see* Fig 31), and then lifts to sweep diagonally up over it, avoiding contact (*see* Fig 32). You could just clip the hair for effect.

'Stopping' Slaps

The slap is stopped or 'pulled', by clenching the striking muscles, just short of the point of impact.

Two contrasting performance styles that use this technique are the following:

1. clown style: where the slap is usually delivered with a straight arm, which, while slower, is more visual. The reaction is exaggerated;
2. theatrical: where a character might employ a sharp but light contact tap to the victim's face (a wake-up, or a challenge, or so on). There is hardly any reaction at all; perhaps just a 'flinch'.

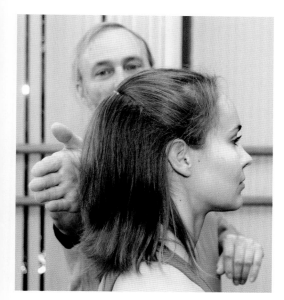

Fig 31

The 'Contact' Slap

A dislocated jaw; a broken nose; concussion; scratches to the ear, eyeball, cheek, nose, lips; displaced contact lenses; a wig sent flying across the stage – these are just some of the delights resulting from a bad contact slap. However, sometimes, a contact slap is not only necessary, but preferable. You may well be asked to do a slap in front of a camera – apparently it brings 'more realism' to the moment. I'll just bet it does!

Contact slaps need considerable trust, timing, confidence and practice, but you should not practise too hard, too often, as your partner's cheek will become very sore indeed.

The first step in the rehearsal technique is to draw your relaxed hand down the cheek of your partner, to sort out the target area and your distance (*see* Fig 33). Do this several times so that your partner gets used to the contact.

Fig 33

I have been on the end of a contact slap in two shows. First (and worst) was from a chap who had very little physical discipline. He 'lost it' in performance; I lost my wig and very nearly the hearing in one ear.

The second (and best) was delivered by a dear friend of mine, whose character in the play had to react to my character's idiocy with a swinging slap. The director insisted that we stage it sideways on to the audience and so a contact slap it had to be. My friend was really unhappy about this but we worked through the technique slowly and surely, and, as our timing improved, she grew in confidence. Three weeks later, in performance, she swung that slap like Zena, Warrior Princess. A marvellous result! Sufficient time for careful practice throughout the rehearsal period, building up to a 'performance speed', gave her the confidence to 'go for it' and I do not remember ever being hurt.

The second step introduces a light diagonal slapping motion, constantly checking with your partner with regard to distance, target and their comfort/pain threshold.

At the third step, you can increase the speed of the delivery of the slap and start to focus, now that you are spot on with distance, target and lightness, on creating a good 'sound effect'.

The victim's reaction is to ride the blow naturally, turning their face away at the moment of impact. However, the victim must be careful not to anticipate the impact. If you turn too soon, you can inadvertently offer a different target and be struck on the ear or the back of the head, or you could cause the attacker to miss completely, defeating the object of a contact slap. Have confidence in your partnership.

Safety note: all slaps, whether contact or non-contact, will need time for practice and rehearsal. Do not allow a director to leave it to the last minute. If something goes wrong that late in the day, the scene leading up to the slap will, in the mind of the actor, be all about how to avoid being hurt again. A director should know better. He does, after all, have a 'duty of care' to his actors.

Tagging a word or two on to 'slap' creates a world of different situations and meanings. How about a 'slapstick situation, where a bit of slap and tickle makes you slap happy. You run slap-bang into your boss, who gives you a slap on the wrist for being late or, if he's in a really bad mood, a slap in the face. Afterwards, your colleagues give you a slap on the back.'

PUNCHES

Until the advent of the Hong-Kong-style martial arts movies and their spectacular kicks, punches were the most common form of unarmed technique used in the Hollywood movies; from 'boxing' jabs to the 'haymakers' of bar-room brawls, from cowboys to *Star Wars*. And the techniques may seem to be as natural as walking, but are they?

In *Overruled* (what George Bernard Shaw called 'A Composition', begun 2 July 1912, completed 23 July 1912), two of Shaw's characters, Gregory Lunn and Sibthorpe Juno, debate a point after Lunn claims that neither of them knows how to fight. According to Juno, 'Every Englishman can use his fists'. Lunn counters, 'Well you're an Englishman, can you use yours?' Juno delivers the stop-hit: 'I presume so. I've never tried.'

Nothing much has changed and most people today have never thrown a punch. Try it,

Fig 34

preferably against a rolled-up gym mat or a punching-bag. It will sort out your technique: the correct way to make a fist, and the way in which the action of the body, in particular from the hips, will give real power to the punch.

To make a fist, roll your fingers into the palm of your hand and then lay your thumb over them, as if to hold them in. Do not tuck your thumb inside your hand, or leave it sticking out; you will only break or dislocate it, if you make contact.

A strong fist may make you want to throw the punch for real, and that is not good stage-fighting technique; should you accidentally

37

Fig 35

Fig 36

Fig 37

make contact, it will hurt both you and your partner. While tight muscles feel powerful, they also inhibit movement. A fast strike can be made only with a relaxed arm and fist. To make a theatrical fist, do not tighten the grip, but leave air between the fingers and the palm of your hand (*see* the middle fist in Fig 34).

There is a wide variety of frequently used punches.

The Cross

David Boushey, Founder of the United Stuntman's Association, Seattle, calls this the 'picture punch', in other words, it is the basic bread-and-butter film punch.

In preparation, the attacker preps high, checking distance with her L. hand (*see* Fig 35). The action involves a straight punch thrown to the 'parrot' (*see* page 26), beside the victim's jaw line, just missing the jaw (*see* Figs 36 and 37). In continuation, the punch falls away. The sound is a victim clap-knap. In reaction, the head turns, following the fist.

The Haymaker

This is a wild swinging punch that levels anything that gets in its way, and requires lots of space between you and your partner. Typically, it is a bar-room brawl punch similar to a Roundhouse (*see* page 40).

Fig 38

Hook

The arm makes the shape of a hook, curved from shoulder to fist (*see* Fig 38). Cue this punch visibly high and keep the curve throughout the punch, making no contact.

Jab to the Face

Straight On

The straight-on jab to the face, a short punch that is snapped forwards, stops a hand's-breadth from the target – the area covering the chin/mouth/nose (*see* Fig 39) – and snaps back. It is never left hanging out there.

Start with both arms bent, close to the body. The jabbing hand is usually the one held in front. From face on, there are two reactions:

1. the victim's head would rock back, as if punched on the nose; however, it is very important to avoid 'crunching' the back of the neck, which can lead to a lot of physiotherapy. There are three things you can do to help: as your head reacts back to the 'hit', think 'up', not 'back'; support the neck muscles by squeezing tight your buttock muscles; add a forward bend of the knees, which allows the back to support the neck, and visually makes the reaction look larger;
2. alternatively, the victim can pull his chin back and down into his neck, as if punched on the jaw.

Fig 39

In the Round

This is used in bare-knuckle boxing, with the back hand held high, almost covering the face (*see* Fig 40). Action: the attacker jabs with her leading hand and makes contact with the victim's 'cupped' hand (*see* Fig 41), which creates the knap. The victim reacts as if he has been hit on the jaw.

Roundhouse

This is a punch that goes 'all around the houses' to reach its target. It is a big swinging blow that can also be 'stopped' for a block, or 'extended' for a duck.

The preparation is a big wind-up out to the side (*see* Fig 42). Action: open the chest wide, allowing the R. to follow (almost like discus throwing).

In terms of distance, for a punch, stay well out of range. If it is to be blocked or ducked, you need to be in distance (*see* Fig 43).

Fig 40

Fig 42

Fig 41

Fig 43

The duck can be developed into a bob and weave (a duck that shifts under the punch, rising on the open side).

Straight Punch

Straight punches vary according to the staging. Below are two examples.

'Pooch Punch'

Physical guru Peppe Ostensson describes this punch as 'stuffing a poodle up a pipe'.

The victim is D.S., back to the audience; the attacker is U.S.R. To gauge the distance, use the windscreen image, imagining that it lies between you.

Fig 45

In preparation, the attacker steps out and 'grabs a stuffed poodle off the shelf' (*see* Fig 42). The victim turns and watches, preparing his hands to clap-knap (*see* Fig 44). Action: the attacker turns her hips, then shoulders to face the L. and, without crossing the line, punches ('pushes the pooch up the pipe'). In reaction, the victim follows the punch with his eyes and face (*see* Fig 45) and clap-knaps as the punch passes in front of him.

The 'Film Punch'

Both fighters are sideways on to the audience, the attacker slightly U.S. of the victim, lining up his R. foot with her R. foot. The attacker's L.

Fig 44

Fig 46

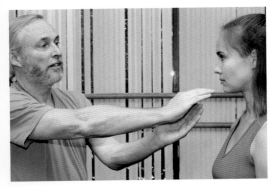

Fig 47

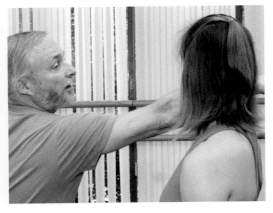

Fig 48

47). Once the knap is made, the punching hand returns to a fist.

In reaction, the victim turns her face to follow the punch (*see* Fig 48). The victim should not anticipate the reaction and turn too soon, in case she offers her jaw or cheekbone as a real target.

Uppercut

Different stagings require different knaps.

Straight Up

Stand directly in front of your partner, out of distance, in a straight U.S./D.S. line. Both partners prepare (*see* Fig 49), the victim's hands lying one on top of the other.

Action: the attacker's open hand swings up, 'clapping' through the victim's. The sound is a shared knap (*see* Fig 50); if not making contact, you could use a victim knap.

Fig 49

Fig 50

hand rests on the outside of the victim's U.S. shoulder. From the audience's P.O.V., the punch is aimed at her face. It will of course pass U.S.

The preparation is high and back, so that it can be clearly seen (*see* Fig 46). Action: launch the punch straight to the 'parrot' (*see* page 26). For the sound, the attacker makes a 'slip-hand' knap. Pull your L. hand back off the victim's U.S. shoulder, on the way striking the fingers against the base of your punching hand, which you have opened slightly (*see* Fig

Fig 51

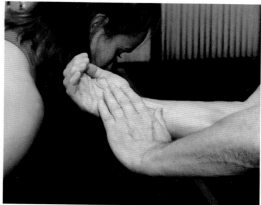

Fig 53

Fig 54

In continuation, the attacker should take care not to curl the punch back in to herself. Think of the 'Olympic Torch'; punch up and lift the 'flame' high, taking the audience's focus up (*see* Figs 51 and 54).

In reaction, once the victim's hands are struck, he should let them fly apart so that the punch can continue on through.

Straight Up but Off to One Side and In Distance

This is my preferred method. It is staged side on to the audience, with the attacker slightly U.S. of the victim, his D.S. foot (R.) in line with the victim's U.S. (R.) foot. His L. hand is on the outside of her U.S. shoulder and his punching hand is in line with it (*see* Fig 52) (U.S. P.O.V.).

For the sound, the attacker's L. hand comes off the victim's shoulder in a slip-hand knap (*see* Fig 53). Continue into the 'Olympic Torch'

Fig 52

(*see* page 43). In her reaction, the victim does not need to knap; her hands are free to go to her face rather than fly away.

Back Fist

Stopped Back Fist
In preparation, the attacker's elbow is pointed at the victim's 'parrot' (*see* Fig 55). Action: extend the fist in a side snap, as if to strike with the knuckles (*see* Fig 56).

Note: let the energy be out and past your partner's face, not into it.

In continuation, 'bounce' the fist a little back off the face. Do not over-extend your arm, as this will hurt; keep it slightly bent.

The victim clap-knaps as her face reacts away from the 'strike' (*see* Fig 57).

Free Back Fist
In form like the backhand slap, the free back fist swings freely through the space between the attacker and the victim, out of distance. The sound is a victim knap.

Fig 56

Fig 55

Fig 57

Upward Back Fist

This is a very filmic punch (*see* Steve Martin in *Roxanne*). In terms of distance, the attacker's L. shoulder is in line with the victim's R. (*see*

Fig 58

Fig 59

Figs 58 and 59 for an indication of the distance between the partners).

In preparation, the attacker lets her arm hang by her side, knuckles forward, then lifts her fist and sees where it ends. The victim adjusts his position until his face is exactly in line with it (*see* Fig 58).

Action: from the elbow, rotate the fist up – the energy of the punch goes upwards to the ceiling. For the knap, the victim could use an inside hand against the thigh. In reaction, the chin is pulled back to the throat, or the head snaps back; the body is allowed to fall away too.

Safety note: do not let the fist go back behind your shoulder and hold it until the victim falls.

Stomach Punch

The Jab to the Stomach

The stance for the attacker is with the R. foot lined up with the victim's U.S. foot (R.), the punching hand in line with the centre of his stomach. To gauge the distance, the attacker can put her L. hand on the victim's R. shoulder or hip (in preparation also to make the knap).

Fig 60

The attacker prepares her fist (*see* Fig 60) and pulls the elbow a little way back. Note that, having established eye contact, she is now focusing on the target. As the partners prepare for the punch, the victim can stretch his hands out towards his attacker, as if to say, 'No, no, don't hit me!'

Action: from the hip, the fist is driven forward in a piston motion. If it is to be a non-contact punch, the attacker stops two inches off the target, adding a little 'bounce' back, as if having struck a solid target. If you have agreed on making contact, just before your fist reaches the target, uncurl your fingers and, with the back of your hand, lightly flick the victim's stomach. As soon as you have made contact, curl the fingers back up, as you pull your fist back out a couple of inches.

Fig 61

With the non-contact punch, there are a couple of ways of making the knap. The attacker can pull her L. hand back as she punches, striking her own body – stomach, hip, leg, wherever is comfortable and unseen. Alternatively, the victim may pull one or both of his hands back on to his own stomach, making sure that they are apart, so that the attacker's fist can pass between them (*see* Fig 61).

Vocally, the victim can use an explosive out-breath, which might cover the knap, making it redundant.

In terms of reaction, the victim can use the force of hitting his own stomach to make him step or jump back, but the most important aspect is where his face goes. His body will contract, or bend over – the extent depends on the force of the blow – but his head should not bend forwards. He could head-butt the attacker, or get hit in the face by her returning fist. The face and head must react in the opposite direction, which is up. Apart from the safety aspect, this is theatre, and the audience wants to see the victim's face reacting to the blow. With this in mind, the victim needs to react up and out into the space D.S. of the punching arm to the audience or towards the camera.

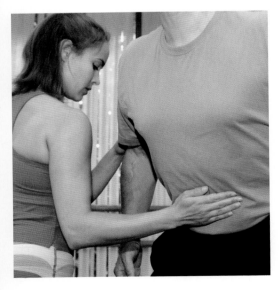

Fig 62

The 'Lay-On'

The attacker adopts her stance, lining up outside the victim, and prepares by pulling her hand back.

Action: she steps forwards on her outside foot, coming alongside the victim, and 'slaps' the fist forwards from the forearm, opening the hand to 'lay' it on the victim's stomach (*see* Fig 62). In reaction, the victim folds over the punch, with an audible out-breath. He may want to go to his knees, using the attacker's arm as a support.

Punch to the Kidney or Back

Distance is established and maintained by the attacker putting his L. hand on the victim's L.

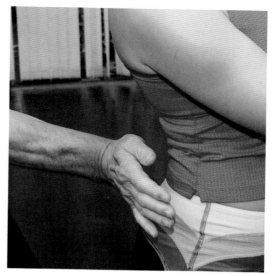

Fig 64

Fig 63

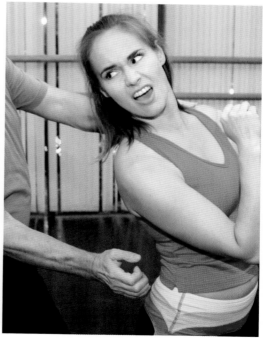

Fig 65

shoulder (*see* Fig 63). Both partners are on balance, knees slightly bent, and the victim can just see the attacker out of the corner of her eye.

Action: the attacker uses his hips to 'launch' the punch.

As with every attack, you have the option to make contact or not. In non-contact, you need to reverse the energy, stopping and 'bouncing' back off, as if you had made contact.

If you have agreed to a contact punch, obviously you must not make contact with her kidneys. Instead, open your hand to make contact with the hip or top buttock muscles (*see* Fig 64).

Reaction: after contact, the attacker's hand returns to a fist and the victim arches away in pain and indignation at the dastardly attack (*see* Fig 65)!

BLOCKS

Blocking creates a shield to stop an attack. In *Star Trek: The Next Generation*, Captain Picard makes a rendezvous with the Romulans at Sector 9, deep in space. The ships arrive together face to face, but they do not arrive together in each other's space – what a mess that would make, and it would only happen once!

The illusion of block is the same: the punch arrives in its own space, and the block arrives simultaneously, in its own space beside it. There is no need for them actually to touch – let alone smash into – each other.

Defender's note: try to block with the muscled parts of your arm, or hands, and avoid bone-on-bone contact; it is 'real', and it hurts.

Attacker's note: punches and kicks should be extended and almost held in suspension for the

Fig 67

Fig 66

Fig 68

Fig 69

ELBOW
Back Elbow to the Stomach
If the actors are directly facing the audience, the attacker (right) stretches out her arm into

Fig 70

block; you should also try to present the muscled part of the arm or leg.

There are a number of different types of block.

Frequently seen in *The Karate Kid* films, half-circle movements are made up or down from the elbow, to block attacks coming straight at you (*see* Fig 66).

Cross-blocks, using the hand or forearm, are used to block across the body, usually in the high line (*see* Fig 67).

Double-hand blocks can also be done with double forearms (the hands clasped together or held apart) (*see* Fig 68).

'X' blocks work equally well against a club or knife attack (*see* Fig 69).

Other 'style' choices include knife-hand blocks, which are done karate style, using the bony edge of the hand. In contrast, Kung-Fu-style blocks are done with the outside of the wrist, the hand opening over the block.

Fig 71

her Fwd. R. diagonal (*see* Fig 70). Action: she pulls her elbow back, but tries to avoid contact with the elbow, which is pointy and bony. There are two options:

1. from a diagonal prep., the elbow is pulled back in and on to the attacker's own side; in effect, she strikes herself (*see* Fig 71);
2. from a straight, forward prep., the elbow is pulled back and the inner side of the upper arm is jammed alongside the rib-cage. This needs more control, for, if you fail to stop your arm, your elbow may still carry through to make contact with your partner.

In reaction, the victim's head goes forwards into the open space (*see* Fig 71; similar to the reaction to the stomach punch).

The sound is provided by the knap – the victim slapping his thigh – or by an appropriate, exaggerated, vocalization.

Choreography note: with a smaller attacker and a larger or stronger victim, just one hit may not be enough to completely break away from the attacker. Try more than one. Clasp hands together to double the apparent force.

Back Elbow to the Chest

This is a sideways strike, with the elbow and upper arm parallel to the ground.

The preparation is made in a forward direction (*see* Fig 72), as if making a R. 'cross'.

Action: for a non-contact strike, pull the arm back from the elbow, out to the side, not back. If making contact, use your triceps on to a chest muscle. Continue to think of pulling the elbow out to the side, not back (*see* Fig 73).

Note: do check that the victim is OK with contact and that they have a muscle area (rather than a breast) to take the hit.

The reaction needs to be marked, as this strike would knock a victim back.

Fig 72

Fig 73

FOREARM

The Double-Forearm Smash to the Back

There are two methods shown here – both 'contact' techniques.

To the 'Body' of the Victim

The attacker prepares by clasping the hands together, without interlocking the fingers, and lifting high (*see* Fig 74).

Action: she brings the hands down, unclasping before contact, and lightly 'slaps' her partner's back, creating the knap (*see* Fig 75).

In continuation, the attacker reverses her energy, and 'bounces' her hands back up in the air, remembering to re-clasp them. In reaction, the victim arches his back.

Fig 75

Fig 74

Fig 76

To the 'Outside' of the Victim's Body
Note: this strike could easily take place with the victim standing up and the attacker striking sideways, in which case she would also prepare sideways.

Action: the attacker's hands strike the outside of the victim's shoulder (*see* Fig 76), continuing on through and re-clasping. The victim reacts by dropping away.

The Double-Forearm Smash to the Stomach

Fig 77

The attacker makes a high and visible prep. (*see* Fig 77).

Action: she swings her arms in to make a light 'contact', and the victim reacts as for the stomach punch (*see* page 45).

The 'Clothes-Line'
This is a wrestling move which now appears in many martial arts films. The attacker runs at the victim, who steps aside, stretching out their arm sideways. The attacker's chest smashes into it and the arm acts as a solid bar to stop the attacker dead; although the attacker's feet continue forwards, the rest of him is going nowhere, and he ends up on his back.

In the movies, an athletic stunt person (like those on Jackie Chan's stunt team), might throw a three-quarter back somersault, to end face down on the floor.

In theatre, as the 'hit' takes place, the victim lets one leg swing forwards and up; hops up on the supporting leg, and then does a back sit-fall (*see* page 106, on the 'total body'). For support, he can take an under-arm grip on to the attacker's outstretched arm.

Safety note: this must be practised with a mat. Do the back sit-fall first, add a jump in to the preparation, then add the attacker's arm to complete the technique.

CHOPS

Karate is the source for the ever-popular (but, by now, almost clichéd) knife-hand attack, used by, among others, Diana Rigg in her all-in-one 'fighting' catsuit in the 1970s British television series *The Avengers*.

The chop is a sharp blow, with the edge of the hand, delivered in a downward angle to the back of the neck. It is also known as the 'rabbit punch', since it reflects the way in which a gamekeeper, having trapped a rabbit in a snare, will put it out of its misery by breaking its neck. Now, we cannot go around putting actors out of their misery, much as we would sometimes like to, so it is necessary to create an illusion.

To the Neck
The attacker prepares by raising her arm at right-angles (*see* Fig 78). Action: she 'chops' down and turns her hand to strike the victim's upper back/lower shoulder muscles, *not* the spine (*see* Fig 79), with the flat of her hand, before 'bouncing' back off with reverse energy. The victim reacts by arching his head and back.

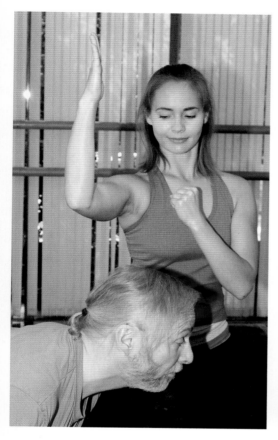

Fig 78

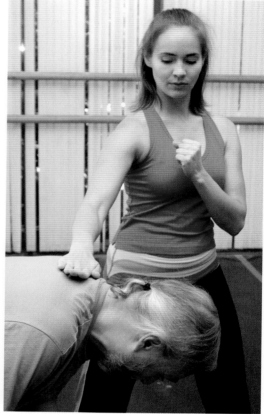

Fig 79

Note: when making contact with a back-hand chop, it may be that the 'chopping' hand turns more comfortably on to its back, particularly if the victim is standing

To the Throat

This was the trademark 'finishing-off' technique used by Billy Two Rivers, a wrestler on British television in the 1960s, who always paraded in to the ring wearing an American Indian headdress.

The attacker prepares by raising her hand, bending at the elbow (*see* Fig 80). Her target is the sternum, just below the line of the collar-bones (*see* Fig 81) for extra safety, to the pectoral muscles on the side of the sternum.

Action: a light 'slap' using reverse energy.

The victim reacts by bringing both hands up to his throat, with arms crossed (*see* Fig 82).

HEAD-BUTTS

Also known as 'nodding with attitude'. Legend has it that 'Does your Granny sew? Well, stitch this!' is a cry that has been heard more than once in a Glasgow street.

Fig 80

Fig 81

Fig 82

The Forehead Attack

The Straight-On Attack

The target, in reality, is the victim's face – forehead, nose or cheek. The move is staged with one partner standing directly in front of the other (*see* Fig 83).

Action: the attacker effects a 'nodding' action (similar to heading a ball towards a goal), stopping short of the victim's partner's face (*see* Fig 84), and 'bouncing off' using reverse energy.

The sound is made by an attacker's knap to the chest.

In reaction, the victim snaps her head back from the 'hit' (*see* also page 39, for the jab in the face). The attacker might also want to show some reaction, as the head-butt is likely to have hurt him too!

Fig 83

Fig 85

With this new angle of attack (*see* Fig 85), the target for the head is the victim's 'parrot', in line with the victim's U.S. ear.

The attacker stands with one foot forward; this will also act as a physical brake to his forward momentum. If the victim is planning to react L. (*see* Fig 87), she should have her R. foot forward.

The preparation is made back in the opposite direction to the strike as above.

Action: eyes now focused on the target (thinking of it not as the victim's nose or forehead but, rather, her cheekbone), the attacker effects a 'nodding' action, with a 'bounce-off'. Whether the attack is straight on or in the diagonal, its effect can be increased by jumping up, and then 'nodding' down. Another method, slightly 'old-fashioned', is for the attacker to stamp his leading foot at the moment of 'contact'.

The sound is made by the victim slapping her U.S. thigh.

Fig 84

The Diagonal Attack
A simple adjustment on to the diagonal for both partners will not only make the forehead attack safer but also heighten the technique dramatically.

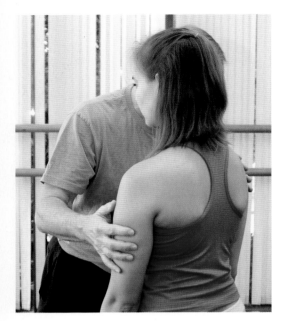

Fig 86

Fig 87

The reaction reflects the 'billiards' or 'bowling-ball' effect, where one ball striking another at an angle causes them both to ricochet off in different directions.

Contact will cause the victim to snap her face away off to the side, towards the audience (or camera), thereby heightening the dramatic effect of the reaction (*see* Fig 87).

Side-of-the-Head Attack

The victim is in a close body grip, and uses this technique as an escape move or a threat, causing the attacker to loosen his grip (not shown).

Back-of-the-Head Attacks

The Standing Backward Attack
The victim is gripped from behind. The victim's target is the face of the attacker, or even his chest, if he towers over you (*see* Fig 92).

Action: a sharp 'backward' blow with the back of the head, but thinking 'up', not 'back'!

In terms of distance, if the attacker is right behind the victim, U.S./D.S., he needs to make sure that his face is back out of distance. It is safer to stand slightly to one side.

The reaction is as for the jab to the face (*see* page 39).

Fig 88

Fig 89

Fig 90

Fig 91

The reaction is similar to Reaction 1 for the Jab to the Face (*see* page 39); think 'up', not 'back' (*see* Fig 91).

Top-of-the-Head Attack

The Upward Attack
The victim's target is the underside of the chin of the person behind her. She needs to stand on balance, close to the chest of the attacker (*see* Fig 92).

Action: having loosened the attacker's grip sufficiently, the victim bends her knees slightly, then, straightening them, 'punches up' with the top of her head, to catch the attacker under the chin (*see* Fig 93).

In terms of reaction, the attacker should be thinking 'up', not 'back'.

The Bent-Over Upward Attack
The victim is gripped from in front (*see* Fig 88).

Action: the victim stands up. The technique for 'real' (*see* Fig 89) works a treat in movies, but in the theatre the 'flight path' of the rising head will be the same as for the upper-cut punch (*see* Fig 90, which shows the actor's P.O.V.).

Fig 92

Fig 93

The Frontal Attack

This is similar to a shoulder barge, but it is the head that seemingly strikes the target – the stomach – and this can be done in a number of ways:

* standing, crouching over (*see* Fig 94);
* charging, as in rugby or American football;
* flying, leaping or diving.

The attacker prepares by stretching the arms forwards, as if intending to grab the victim.

Action: the attacker uses his legs to drive the attack, ending with a lunge in on the front leg (which also acts as a brake). His hands reach to the hips of his partner (*see* Fig 95).

In reaction, the victim helps to brake the action by stepping back a pace or more, while

Fig 94

Fig 95

The victim then uses both hands to push his head up and back, as if bouncing off the wall. He could also jam a foot against the bottom of the wall, creating three points of contact, but he should try to avoid actually kicking the wall.

Reactions may involve a fall away, or he could turn, lean back against the wall, then slide down it to the floor (watching out for any hooks, nails, or wood fastenings such as skirting boards).

Walking into a Door

If the door is shut, the same principle applies as for the wall. However, a nice comic touch is to begin to open the door, and then to bash your face into it, as if you had pulled the door into your face.

bending over from the energy of the attack and placing her hands on the attacker's back. This will help keep her face up to avoid banging her chin on the attacker's back.

HEAD OR FACE SLAMS

For the victim, the action of 'bouncing off' an object can be performed from running, walking, standing, sitting, kneeling or lying on the floor; the same principles will apply.

Safety note: while the attacker may initiate or appear to lead, it is the victim who actually controls the action. The attacker should never, at any time, push the victim's head or body during these moves.

Running into a Wall

At the moment of impact, the victim stops himself with his hands – one hand at chest or waist height (wherever comfortable) acting as a brake (*see* Fig 96). The other hand will make contact with the wall to prevent his face hitting it. This creates the knap.

Fig 96

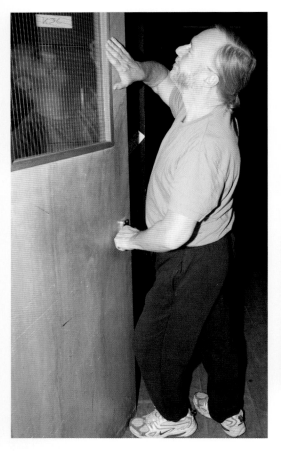

Fig 97

Fig 98

If the door opens towards you (arcing to your L.) with its handle on the R. edge – open the door with your L. hand, use your L. foot to block it, and with your R. hand, slap the door at face height (*see* Fig 97), creating the knap. If the door opens the other way, to your R., reverse the process.

Both knap and reaction – 'bouncing back' off the solid object – will sell this technique.

Sitting

The cue involves the attacker laying his hands on the victim's head and U.S. shoulder (*see* Fig 98). In preparation, the victim leans back, raising her arms for the knap, takes a breath and then moves into the action (*see* Fig 99).

Action: the partners move together, the attacker's forward 'push' going over the top of the victim's head (*see* Fig 100). The victim takes her head down to within a few centimetres of the table top, slamming her hands on to the table to create the sound, and to give her the energy to push back off in re action.

In reaction, the victim comes back off the table, holding her head 'in pain'.

Kneeling

The victim prepares by finding her balance (*see* Fig 101). As the attacker 'lifts' her up and

Fig 99

back, she takes a breath, and then the attacker launches into action.

Action: the attacker begins a 'forward' movement with his body as well as his hands (*see* Fig 102). The victim curls forwards, striking one or both hands on the floor to create the knap and to help her 'bounce' up and off the floor. Then, in reaction to the 'hit', she slumps forwards (*see* Fig 103).

Lying Down

This move definitely requires more strength and effort from the victim, as she has to take all her own weight on her L. hand and arm (*see* Fig 104). In preparation, she pushes herself

Fig 100

Fig 101

Fig 102

Fig 103

up, raising her R. hand in reaction to the 'pull-back', preparing to knap.

Action: the attacker's energy goes 'forwards', over the top of the victim's head (*see* Fig 105). She takes it down to within several centimetres of the floor, slamming her R. hand on to the floor to make the knap.

The victim firmly supports her upper body in the 'bounce-off' reaction, before slumping to the floor as above.

Chair Slams

In the Face
The attacker prepares by lifting the chair with the seat pointing straight at the victim's face (*see* Fig 106).

Action: he steps in, moving the chair forward in a straight line, strongly stopping himself and the chair (*see* Fig 107). The victim could just as easily have walked towards a stationary attacker.

Note: do not swing the chair in a curve, in case you hit your partner with its leading edge.

For the knap, the victim brings up her hands to slap the momentarily stationary chair, with her face centimetres away from the seat. She reacts by backing off with her head (thinking 'up', not 'back'), as if the chair seat had struck her face; at the same time, the attacker pulls the chair back away, as if 'bouncing' it off her face.

In terms of staging, the attacker is D.S. with his back to the audience, and the victim is U.S.,

Fig 104

Fig 105

Fig 106

Fig 107

so that her face disappears out of view for a moment behind the back of the chair.

On to the Head

This uses a similar technique to the chair slam to the face, but it is delivered from a different angle (*see* Fig 108). Also, the attacker uses a different grip, to assist the bounce-off in an upward direction.

The victim may react either as above, or she could turn to face the audience (reflecting the 'billiard-ball' effect, *see* Fig 87, page 56).

Staging note: the move is shown here staged on the diagonal, to make it easier to see the

Fig 108

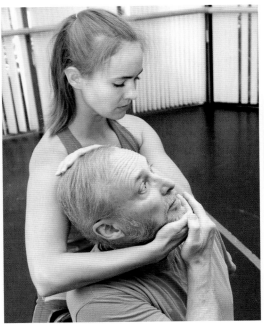

Fig 109

technique, but it works more effectively if the attacker is directly U.S. of the victim, who has her back to the audience.

This technique could easily be used by a smaller person standing on a table, a tree or a rock and striking down on another; one example might be Peter Pan attacking Captain Hook.

Other Weapons
This 'slam' technique can be adapted for use with any kind of 'whacking' object, including a tray, a pillow, a club, and a plank (as in a pantomime routine).

NECK BREAK

The situation is that the attacker is behind the victim, her body acting as a support, and one hand lightly cupping the victim's chin. The other rests on top of the victim's head, as if to lock it down.

Fig 110

The victim reaches round with his front hand – as if to hold and prevent – placing it on top of the attacker's hand. The victim 'leads' (controls the whole action) by 'winding up' to the L. (*see* Fig 109); he takes a breath and prepares himself for the action.

Action: the victim turns his head R. in the direction of the break, pulling the attacker's hand, which rests lightly on his chin, off and away (*see* Fig 110). The top half of the attacker's body twists in the same direction, giving the illusion of the kind of force necessary to break the victim's neck.

The sound may be made in a couple of ways:

❋ with his free hand, the victim could try snapping his fingers in the 'Spanish' style;
❋ popping bubble wrap can make a sound like vertebra being torn and snapped. The victim would have to use both hands behind his back, trusting his attacker to release on cue, and not to actually pull his chin around. He should twist the bubble wrap as he turns his head.

The victim's reaction is to collapse; an inward crumple, like a puppet that has had its strings cut, will be more effective than a straight fall. The victim could lean against the attacker's body as he slides to the floor.

Safety note: both partners need to be strongly on balance throughout this technique. Whether he is standing, sitting or kneeling, the victim of the broken neck will have to 'slump' as if dead, and he will not want to pull the attacker over on top of him, thereby risking being hurt.

STRANGLES

A strangle is the action of squeezing the windpipe or neck, using either both hands or just one. This is a contact situation in which the partners are up close and personal, and the

Some actors are particularly sensitive around the neck and when anyone tries the strangle technique on them, they either start away or burst into giggles. This reaction might prove to be unfortunate if such an actor were to play, for example, Desdemona; Othello would not get quite the reaction he was expecting when trying to 'Put out the light...'.

attacker's hands are around the other's throat. However, at no time is there any actual squeezing of the victim's neck.

From the Front

The Standing Strangle
In preparation, the attacker reaches out to his victim, who is recoiling in terror and stretching out her arms to ward off the attack (*see* Fig 111). In fact, in stage-fighting the reverse is happening. She is actually reaching out to grab the attacker's wrists and guide his hands towards (but not on to) her throat. The attacker can use either the neck grab or the jaw grab.

When employing the neck grab, the heels of the attacker's hands are on the victim's

Fig 111

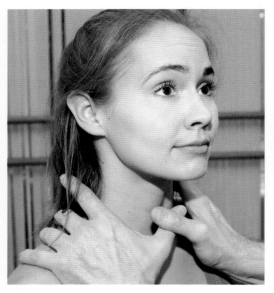

Fig 112

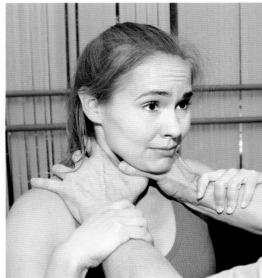

Fig 113

collar-bones, little fingers gripping the shoulders (*see* Fig 112). The forefingers need to be completely relaxed, as they are very close to the carotid arteries and the jugular veins in the side of her neck. The attacker's thumbs are pressing back into each other, not pressing into the victim's throat, where they could cause damage by crushing the windpipe or voice box.

The victim completes the illusion by stretching out her neck and lowering her chin on to my thumbs, closing the obvious gap, or 'hiding

Jenn Zuko Boughn, in her book *Stage Combat*, delightfully describes the action of stretching out the neck and lowering the chin as 'turtling the chin'. It is a constant challenge for teachers to come up with descriptions or images to which their students can relate, and use as an *aide-memoire* – I love this one!

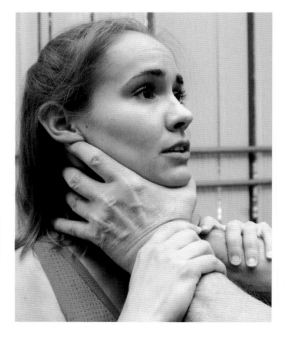

Fig 114

the air' (*see* Fig 113). She also has a firm grip on the attacker's wrists, holding them down on to her upper chest.

Action: the tension of the 'strangle' is created by reversing the energy. The attacker tries to pull his hands away, while the victim holds the attacker's hands in place.

The alternative hand grip is the jaw grab (*see* Fig 114), with the attacker's thumb and forefinger holding the victim's jaw-line, creating a 'hollow' grip with no contact on the front of her throat. The victim maintains control of the grip by holding the attacker's wrists, as she presses her jaw down into his hands.

The Lying Strangle
It is much easier to work on the floor, as the victim is supported, for training purposes, by the mat.

Action: the grip is the same as for the standing strangle. The victim is holding the attacker's hands in place while she 'strangles'

Fig 116

him, using reverse energy to pull away. Notice that the attacker is using her L. leg, not only to support her own weight but also to 'push' herself away. You can, of course, kneel across your victim but it is still a good idea to have one knee up to support your weight, and to prevent you from falling forwards on to the victim (*see* Fig 115). This is especially important if they thrash around – strangling is known to lead to a terrifying sensation of 'air hunger' and may induce violent struggling. The victim should try to do most of his thrashing about with his legs, keeping the upper half of his body reasonably still, to avoid putting too much strain on the 'grip' around his throat. He should also remember that his movements will grow weaker as his time runs out.

Fig 115

The Lifted Strangle

This front strangle, using one or two hands, can be taken into a lift, free-standing or against a wall. 'Charles the Wrestler' in Shakespeare's *As You Like It* is one character who may well use such a move.

In the one-hand jaw grip (*see* Fig 117), the other hand is actually supporting the victim, holding her R. foot. She is putting her weight on the convenient ballet bar, but she is also maintaining a very firm two-handed grip on the wrist of the attacker's throttling hand. The victim can also support herself by standing on the attacker's thighs or, sitting and gripping with her own thighs, on either side of the attacker's chest.

Fig 117

The Kill

Death by strangulation occurs as a result of 'squeezing' the blood vessels, the carotid arteries and jugular veins in the side of the neck, stopping oxygen, via the blood, from getting to the brain.

In reality, when the attacker squeezes, the victim's first reaction is to try to grab whatever is around his throat (Stage 1). As this fails, he tries to grab the strangler (Stage 2). Last, as he fails to dislodge the attacker, on the edge of falling into the darkness, like a swimmer underwater trying to reach the surface, he reaches impotently for air (Stage 3) (*see* Fig 116).

Strangulation techniques in, for example, judo, can cause unconsciousness in 8 to 14 seconds. Apparently, when the hands are released, the subject will regain consciousness in about twice the length of time that he was under.

Safety note: do *not* try this at home.

After the victim has reached a state of unconsciousness, it will still take the brain another four minutes or more to die from lack of oxygenated blood. In a theatrical strangle, the audience will have gone home if you hang on to the victim's neck for four minutes, so use the time it takes to slip into unconsciousness – say, 12 seconds overall – as your time-frame to complete the three stages of the theatrical kill.

Having the victim's hands waving in the air just before he 'dies' increases the 'death reaction'. On camera, there may be a turn of the head, a sigh, or a slight widening of the eyes. On stage, the victim may well turn his head, but his attacker is usually hunched over his body, hiding him from the audience. To make it an obvious death, the victim can let his hands reach up, pause and then fall.

THROTTLES: THE SLEEPER HOLD

Choke holds, or 'constriction techniques', usually require less strength than brute-force hands-on strangling, so are generally considered superior.

The sleeper hold is also called the 'lateral vascular neck restraint' and is apparently widely taught in law enforcement. In a real situation (*see* Fig 118), the attacker's hands would be gripping each other, for greater 'squeezing power'. This is not the case in the stage combat version, which is performed as follows:

1. The attacker stands behind and close to the R. side of his partner, supporting her body with his leading hip and chest.

Fig 119

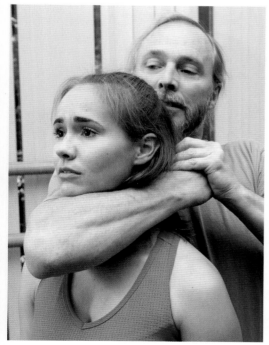

Fig 118

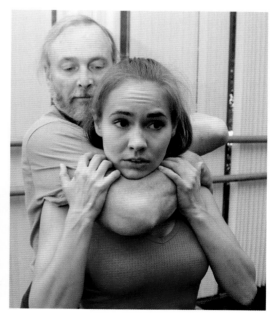

Fig 120

2. With his R. hand, he reaches around his partner's neck and places it on her L shoulder (*see* Fig 119). This should keep his elbow comfortably clear of her throat. If the attacker is taller, his R. armpit will rest on the top of the victim's R. shoulder (*see* Fig 120). This is the main grip, but it needs securing.
3. With his L. hand gripping the victim's R. shoulder, the attacker firmly presses his L. forearm against the victim's upper back. The attacker exerts no pressure. The victim holds on to the attacker's R. forearm.

Safety note: the victim should ensure that her throat is safely in the 'V' of the attacker's forearm, closing the obvious gap by 'turtling' her chin forwards (*see* page 66).

Following a sleeper hold, the victim's reaction is to lapse, after a brief struggle using the 8–14-second guide, into 'unconsciousness'.

Helpful hints: the attacker should make sure not to drop the victim. If, in the struggle, the victim has not already gone to the ground, the attacker should lower her down before laying her out. The victim will need to hang on with her hands for support as the attacker lays her down, protecting her throat at the same time.

THE GARROTTE

Holding a strangle for four or more minutes is impractical and tiring. An object such as a rope, scarf, or cord initially used to induce unconsciousness, can be tied around the neck to cut off the blood flow permanently.

The Reverse Strangle

The attacker has attacked from behind, wrapping a scarf around the victim's throat. She then steps in with a half-turn, placing her backside against mine (as in a Judo throw), and 'takes up the slack'. With one hand between his throat and the scarf, the victim obligingly leans back as far as possible, maintaining his balance and remaining in control of his weight (*see* Fig 121).

A network of robbers and assassins in India called the Thuggees used to strangle their victims by throwing a yellow scarf, symbolic of the Hindu Goddess Kali, around their throat (garrotte). Subsequently, during the British Imperial Rule in India, the term 'thug', like so many other 'Indian' words, became part of common English.

Fig 121

Using a Noose

If using a noose with a slip-knot, you need to find a way of securing the knot so it does not tighten at any cost; you may not have the added safety of the victim's hands to protect his airways (if he is tied up or held).

Start by placing the noose around the victim's neck and establish a comfortable size of loop (not skin-tight). Make a mark where the knot is, on the bit of rope that slides and tightens. Now tie a tight knot on that mark. When you tighten the noose again, the rope should stop at the knot and be unable to tighten any further.

With a Cutting Object

If the garotte is made from wire, it will cut deeply into the neck, causing the victim to bleed out, which does not take as long as strangulation. Obviously, for stage combat wire is not used. When using rope, it is possible to simulate the bleeding from the neck by means of a thin tube with small holes pricked around its centre. This is connected to two handles, hollowed out and filled with 'blood'; when squeezed, the 'blood' is forced down the tube, and out of the holes. This method is used in *Death-Trap* by Ira Levin; the actor is also required to shoot a crossbow on stage!

RESTRAINTS

These are techniques that control and limit the victim's movement.

The Head-Lock

The attacker stands to one side of the victim, with both partners facing the same way. As he curls his R. arm around the victim's neck, the victim is 'forced' to bend at the waist. The attacker now places his fist on his R. hip. To 'reinforce' the lock, his L. hand is brought across to take hold of his R. wrist.

As in the strangle technique, the victim acts as follows:

* Step 1: bring up your outside arm and place your hand on the 'locking' forearm, making sure your airway is clear by turning your head to face in towards your attacker.
* Step 2: wrap your inside arm around the attacker's waist to hold and support yourself.

The Full Nelson

Standing behind the victim, the attacker places his arms under her armpits, then curls them up to place his hands, one on top of the other, not clasped, behind her neck (*see* Fig 122).

Safety note: locked fingers are more difficult to pull apart or release quickly, should the victim need to escape the grip.

Fig 122

Fig 123

Action: in a real situation, the attacker would now press down on the victim's neck to restrain him. In the theatrical context, the energy is reversed; the victim presses her head back against the attacker's hands, which creates the 'tension and pressure'.

The Hammer-Lock

A single-arm restraining hold, where one of the victim's arms is pushed up and held behind his back.

The attacker loosely grasps the victim's wrist. The victim takes control of the action by twisting his own arm and placing it up behind his back (the safest place being the middle). In continuation, the attacker moves around the victim, and places her other hand on to his opposite shoulder.

In reaction, the victim – in response to the attacker 'pushing up' his arm – rises up on to his toes. He may place his free hand on to his shoulder, as if the shoulder socket is really painful, while leaning in that direction – favouring the injury (*see* Fig 123).

> The 'ghostly attack' was a favourite movie gag, notably performed as *Blackbeard's Ghost* by Peter Ustinov. Neither the victim, nor the audience, sees the 'ghost', but, by performing all of the reactions – hand up the back, up on the toes, leaning over towards the shoulder with the free hand on it – the actor can make the audience believe that he is being pushed around by some nasty spirit.

HAIR/EAR/NOSE PULLS

The Hair Pull

Standing

The attacker prepares by approaching the victim's head from above and to one side with his hand. This should be made clearly visible to his partner as well as to the audience (*see* Fig 124).

The first step for the attacker is to place the hand in the victim's hair, and curl it, as if gripping it. The ends of the fingers are turned over, like a 'paw', so that the attacker's fingernails do not dig into the victim's scalp. There should still be 'air' between his grip and the victim's hair (*see* Fig 125). The victim can control the attack from the start by bringing her hands up, gripping the attacker's wrist, and guiding his hand into position on her head. Alternatively, once his hand is in place, she can put one of hers on the back of his palm, not the knuckles, and the other on his wrist (*see* Fig 126).

The second step is to secure the grip. As the attacker's grip is empty, it can easily fall away; the victim must pull the attacker's hand down

Fig 124

Fig 125

firmly on to her head, at the same time freeing her neck muscles so that her head can move around as if reacting to the hair pull.

Safety note: the victim needs to keep her elbows up so she can see where she is going. The audience also wants to see the victim's face and hear her dialogue and/or screams.

The third step is to introduce some movement. Moving the victim around using the above grip puts a big strain on the victim. The attacker uses his free hand to clasp her leading forearm, and uses that to pull, or, more accurately, guide, her around until it is time for the release. (*See* Fig 126; assume that the attacker has his R. hand on her head in the same grip. His L. hand can now grasp her R. forearm for the 'pull-around'.)

Safety note: do not pull your victim around for ever, as they can get very disorientated. Pull a little, then stand and shake (as in the exercise; *see* below), pull a little more, and so on.

Vocals are very important. The victim screaming, as she is dragged around, really colours the whole effect. When the attacker is standing still and she is not screaming, he can then deliver his dialogue.

Fig 126

The release should always be controlled and rehearsed.

Hair Pull-and-Release Exercise

* Preparation: both partners stand still, feet comfortably apart, and establish the hair-pull position.
* Exercise: the victim leans to one side, then to the other and, finally, comes back to centre. She bends forwards slightly, and then, straightening her legs, throws her arms and head up, 'releasing the attacker's hold'. Victim-control here means that she leads and the attacker will follow.
* Note: the victim must come back to centre before the 'bend-and-release'. The attacker must stand to one side so he does not get head-butted on the 'release'.

The Floor Drag

This is typical 'caveman' tactics. The attacker has a good handful of the victim's hair and she has a very good grip of my arm (*see* Fig 127). The 'drag' is accomplished by the victim using her legs to push herself along, supporting her own body weight by holding on tight (*see* Fig 128). The attacker simply walks away.

In a movie, the actor would probably wear a body harness, with stirrups under her feet. A wire attached to the back of the harness near her neck would be taken up through her hair, along the attacker's arm, and through his costume. She could just lie back 'unconscious' and allow herself to be dragged.

The Ear Pull

Using the same technique as for the hair pull, the attacker places her cupped hand as if to grasp the other's ear. The victim immediately grabs her wrist and pulls in to keep her hand on (*see* Fig 129).

Fig 127

Fig 128

The Nose Pull

The attacker has bent her first two fingers so that the middle phalanges rest up against the inner part of the victim's cheekbones (*see* Fig 130). In preparation, using victim-control, the victim has already grasped the attacker's wrist and placed her hand.

Action: the victim needs to keep the attacker's hand pressed up against his face, to stop it falling away – she is not gripping, after all. If she leads the victim, he follows, maintaining the pressure so that her hand cannot escape.

The release is done in clown style, and goes as follows: the attacker lifts her free hand up between the partners, then 'slaps' down on to the back of her own hand, letting it fall away. As her hand descends, the victim releases his grip, and then reacts as if she has slapped down on to his nose. If the attacker rises up on to her toes during the preparation, this would appear to add power to the effect. Jumping up before slapping down would add a nice 'comedic' touch.

SCRATCHES

The last thing you want to do is actually scratch your partner with your fingernails. Can they be cut? If not, try the following method.

The attacker has brought her hand in from the side and curled her fingers under, just before placing the flat, middle part of her fingers on the victim's cheek (*see* Fig 131). To simulate the scratch, she pulls the heel of her hand through, back towards the opposite side

Fig 130

Fig 131

Fig 132

of her body, allowing the wrist joint to bend in. During the action, the flat parts of her fingers will slide safely and smoothly down the victim's cheek. She needs to take care not to cock the knuckles forwards as this will put pressure on to the cheek.

The victim will naturally react by turning his head with the 'scratch', before the attacker's fingers reach his chin.

Alternatively, if the attacker's fingernails are short, she can try resting the pads of her fingers on the victim's face (*see* Fig 132). The action is as above: pulling the heel of the hand down, through and back.

Safety note: whichever method you choose, keep your thumb back as you perform the scratching action. Do not allow it to curl and hook in to your partner's cheek.

If there has to be blood drawn from the scratch, the attacker (using the second method) could put some blood on her fingertips before 'scratching'. Alternatively, the victim could have a sponge lightly soaked in stage blood in a pocket (in a freezer bag) and, as he brings his hand up to cover his face in reaction, he can place the blood himself.

BITES

You can bite anything you want – with some provisos.

In preparation, the attacker can show the audience her teeth (watch any Dracula movie for tips on how to do this; *see* Fig 133). The action is either to lay her lips on the target and 'gum' instead of 'bite', or to bite her own thumb (out of sight), as it grips the victim's forearm.

As the victim reacts visually and vocally, he needs to take care not to move his arm around, as this might damage his partner's teeth.

The attacker, having 'bitten', pulls the mouth away, re-showing the teeth, as the victim covers the supposed bite in reaction.

Fig 133

KICKS

Kicks can be delivered from any position, even lying down, and usually take one of two forms:

1. the 'free' kick, which is out of distance and makes no contact;
2. the contact kick, which is in distance and makes contact with either the hands in lieu of the face, or a muscled body part such as the stomach, thigh or buttock.

Helpful hints: if a victim is repeatedly taking 'strikes' to the hands while rehearsing, it is a good idea to wear gloves.

General Notes

* Snap kicks: made with the top (shoe-laces) of a relaxed foot; a good rule of thumb is 'slow in and fast out'.
* Thrust kicks: made with the ball of the foot or the flat.
* Preparation for both: lift the knee before kicking.
* Swung kicks: from the thigh, with the whole leg.
* Contact kicks should be light and snapped back. With practice, they can be so controlled that only the attacker's shoe-laces make contact!
* Staging: contact kicks do not need to be hidden; for non-contact kicks, use the U.S./D.S. line or the diagonals to hide the 'air' from the audience.
* Knaps: contact kicks create their own knap; non-contact kicks need a body/clap-knap.
* Vocals: can hide the lack of knap or add to the overall effect.

Safety note: the kicker needs to warm up his legs first with good stretches. It is very easy to pull a hamstring muscle when kicking.

Free Kicks

Snap Kick to the Face

A non-contact kick with one partner back to the audience; on the U.S./D.S. line, and out of distance (*see* Fig 134). This kick could also be staged sideways on to the audience with the attacker's kick (in distance) going U.S. of the victim.

Crescent Kick

Crescent kicks are non-contact kicks, with a flexed foot, sweeping inwards or outwards, usually made with the front foot (*see* Fig 135).

Fig 134

They form a perfect arc, 'contacting' at the height of the kick.

There is an exception: the reverse spin kick, which uses the back foot and was described by Bruce Lee in the film *The Way of the Dragon* as 'dragon whips his tail'.

Helpful hints: try 'sweeping' your leg over the back of a chair.

Versions of crescent kicks are frequently seen in street dancing and in the Brazilian art of capoeira.

INWARD CRESCENT

Take a step out to the side, and then sweep that leg inwards, up and over in an arc. When you land on the other side you have three options (practise them all):

1. pull the leg straight back to your starting position;
2. step on to the ball of your front foot and pivot your body all the way round to your starting position (*see* Fig 136);
3. do another kick, returning the way you came or, stepping on to it, doing a spin and reverse kick.

Fig 135

Fig 136

OUTWARD CRESCENT

Take a small step to the Back R. 45 degrees, then sweep that leg diagonally into the Fwd. L. 45 degrees, before arcing up and over to your R. (outwards).

REVERSE SPIN

Step diagonally across in front of your kicking foot, pivoting the heel forwards. Now, using your arms to counter-balance and your hips for power, twist your body around, letting your back leg whip up and over. The momentum will be great, so watch your balance.

The general reaction to all the crescent kicks is a marked one, as their power will 'whip' the victim's face around, followed by his body (*see* the victim in Fig 136). To build the reaction, the victim can add a fall; a spin or two into a fall; a step into a forward roll or a forward flip over on to his back. If he is particularly gymnastic, or 'wired', he could throw in a forward somersault. Watch kung fu movies for inspiration, particularly those featuring Jackie Chan and his stunt team.

The Banana Kick

This is a kick to the face of a victim lying on their side. The old-fashioned way of simulating contact is for the victim to leave out a cupped hand for the kicker to target, using the shoe-lace (top) of his foot as his leg sweeps through. The potential for damage to the hand is great, so it might be preferable not to make contact, and allow the attacker to kick freely.

The attacker prepares, keeping well U.S. (*see* Fig 137), and taking care not to let his kicking foot get too close to the victim's face. It is very scary for the victim.

Fig 137

Fig 138

Action: the attacker moves in (stepping or running) and plants his supporting foot clearly U.S. of, but in line with, the victim's head (as if preparing to kick a football). Then he 'sweeps' his kicking leg through, letting it curve away from the victim – hence the name 'banana'.

The victim reacts by throwing her arms and head up along the mat, and arching her body (*see* Fig 138). Such is the force of this kick, that, at the very least, the victim will roll over on to her back; even better, she might roll right over to face the audience. The reaction can be heightened further by adding a roll or two.

Special effect: if the victim ends up facing the audience, it is an ideal opportunity to spit out blood and the odd broken tooth. Use a blood capsule and bits of Polo mint, put in your mouth while lying facing U.S.

Kicks to the Body

Side Snap
If the kick is to make contact, the target is the stomach muscles. If there is to be no contact you can include the face or head as well.

In terms of staging, the attacker stands sideways on to the victim. In terms of distance, the top of the foot (the shoe-laces) should line up with the centre of the target.

Fig 139

Note: the attacker's L. hand grasps the R. hand of the victim, to gauge distance and to help her balance (*see* Fig 139).

The attacker preps her R. foot back, stepping on to her L. foot, and 'cocking' her R. knee high.

Action: the attacker swivels the L. heel towards the victim, snapping the kicking foot towards the target. If desired, a light contact may be made, then the foot is snapped back off, and returned to the floor (pivoting the heel of the supporting foot back as well).

Standing Facing

This contact snap kick is in distance, with a shared knap (*see* Fig 140).

In preparation, the attacker steps on to the supporting leg, lifting the kicking knee up in front of her. Action: she snaps the kick forward – not up – with her toes extended.

A blow to the stomach will bend the victim over, but, in reacting, he should endeavour to keep his face up.

This kick is also effective with the victim kneeling. The victim kneels on the R. (U.S.) knee, L. knee up. The attacker kicks through his hands, aiming at his R. (U.S.) 'parrot'. In reaction, the victim swivels to the R. and falls.

Fig 141

Standing Facing – Side Thrust

This kick aims to make contact with the stomach or chest; it may also delivered to the back muscles.

In preparation, the attacker turns her supporting foot sideways as she steps on to it, turning her body as she lifts her kicking knee.

Action: she pivots her supporting heel towards the target, thrusting the edge of her kicking foot out. She counter-balances by leaning her body away in the opposite direction (*see* Fig 141).

For the victim, this is as much a 'pushing' kick as it is a 'punching' one, and he reacts by being knocked back as well as folded over. In films, the victim sometimes has a wire (a jerk harness) attached, to make him fly back, creating a highly exaggerated but excellent reaction.

Kneeling Sideways

This can be carried out with or without contact.

Before you start, you need to examine where your partner's ribs end and the hip-bone

Fig 140

Fig 142

can exaggerate this lifting movement by raising her arms with her knee – more *West Side Story* in style than *The Godfather*.

The victim will certainly be 'winded' by the kick, and his reaction may be to crumple to the floor (as in *Superman Returns*) or he could be lifted up and over on to his back and into a sideways roll (as seen in *Tomb Raider*). In the latter case, the victim needs to anticipate the reaction by pushing off with his hand and leg nearest to the attacker (*see* Fig 142).

Safety note: it is very important for the victim to keep his stomach muscles tight during this technique, to prevent him being winded should the kick land too hard.

The Step-Over

This non-contact kick is a particular favourite of fellow fight director Steve Wilsher.

The situation is that the victim is lying down on the floor, with her back to the attacker. The attacker prepares by stepping up close, lifting his kicking leg up over her (*see* Fig 143).

Action: the leg is brought down by gravity, and the victim is struck in the stomach by the heel of the attacker's foot.

Safety note: the attacker must make sure that his foot lands about 30cm (12in) clear in front of his partner's stomach, and that his calf muscle does not impact with her rib-cage. The victim should lean back a little as the attacker's foot descends, as if to get a clearer look.

According to Steve Wilsher, the kick appears more vicious if the attacker keeps his eyes fixed firmly forwards throughout the technique, only taking in the victim peripherally.

In reaction, the victim 'ooofs' and jack-knifes in around the attacker's leg (*see* Fig 144).

In continuation, the attacker can either pull the leg back out, effectively rolling the victim on to her back, or step over and walk forwards away from the victim.

begins. The gap is not very wide, so the victim should push back the leg nearest the kicker a hand's breadth, to open up the target area a little more.

If the attacker is kicking with her R. leg, her partner should be facing to her L. and at right-angles. Most kicks tend to swerve in a little (banana style) as the leg swings forward, and you do not want the toe of the attacker's foot swerving into the victim's crotch area. The attacker lines up her L. foot opposite the victim's L. shoulder, and kicks straight to his stomach.

Action: the kick may be snapped in and under to make contact. Alternatively, the attacker can swing her leg in and, just as it makes contact, lift the knee up high. Her foot will then brush her partner's side. The attacker

Fig 143

Kick to the Thigh – Victim Facing Away
Whether it makes contact or not, this is a kick to collapse the leg, as if having struck the knee joint. The victim makes a half-lunge to the side, to make sure that he 'presents' a good target: the muscles in the back of the thigh of the bent leg, midway between the knee and the crotch. If the attacker is a R.-footed kicker, the victim should step out with his L. (*see* Fig 145) (and vice versa).

The attacker prepares by taking a small step out to the L. and, angling her body slightly to that side, lifts her knee at a right-angle to the target.

Action: snap-kick in to the back of the victim's L. thigh and snap out.

In reaction, the victim's leg, bending from the knee, will 'collapse' as a result of the blow.

Kick to the Thigh – Victim Facing You
In every other respect, this is the same as above.

Note: the attacker must make absolutely sure of the target, which lies between the knee

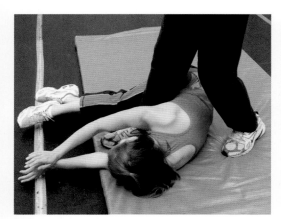

Fig 144

Fig 145

Fig 146

thrusting his hips forwards and then tilting up. This will lift the 'sensitive bits' up out of the way.

Action: if the victim is taller than the attacker, the attacker will not need to compensate so much. If she is shorter, she will need to bend her supporting leg as she begins her snap kick with a relaxed extended foot. She should make contact with the victim's buttocks with her shoe-lace area.

Note: the attacker bends the supporting leg to prevent her shin-bone from making contact with the victim's crotch.

Fig 147

and the crotch (*see* Fig 146). If she stands too far L. the kick will slide up the victim's leg into the crotch; too far to the R. and her kick will curve into her partner's knee. Ouch!

Groin Kick
The fake or illusional kick to the crotch can be made to the inside thigh muscle, exactly the same as above. The victim, reacting to the pain, grabs his crotch rather than his knee, directing the audience's focus there.

The kick 'right up the middle' (referred to in Jenn Zuko Boughn's book as the 'British groin kick') aims to reach under the victim's crotch and strike the centre of the buttocks (*see* Fig 147). (It can be angled to strike only one buttock.)

The attacker prepares for this low snap kick by standing to the L. of the victim with her R. kicking leg on a line 'right up the middle'. The victim stands with his legs open and 'presents' the target by tucking his tailbone under, or

In continuation, the attacker should make sure that she snaps her leg back out (although there are exceptions to this rule – *see* below.)

Winter 2006, Northcott Theatre, Exeter. In the pantomime *Aladdin*, there was a feisty 6-foot giant panda who, in one of the action sequences, ended his attack with a mighty crotch kick. Mid-kick, we had the victim, Handy Andy, close his legs 'in pain', trapping the Panda's leg straight up the middle, much to the amusement of the children in the audience. Whilst giving the audience time to 'appreciate' the kick, trapping the leg also gave both actors more control over the technique and the comedy moment.

Fig 148

The sound will be provided by the 'contact', which will create a satisfying knap. Vocals are also very important.

Normally, the victim will react by closing his thighs quickly, bringing his hands immediately into that extremely sensitive area. The damage could be so severe that he will be 'incapable of doing anything further', which is why crotch kicks should be kept to the end of the fight.

Kick to the Thigh – Victim Lying Down
This is a contact kick, performed in the same way as if the victim were standing up. The victim needs to present a good target, then the attacker steps in and snaps the kick in and out, lightly but accurately (*see* Fig 148).

The victim will react by closing his legs fast 'in pain' and will probably roll over on to his side; the attacker needs to make sure that she steps well clear.

Kick Along the Thigh – Victim Lying Down
This is a contact kick, with the attacker grabbing the victim's outstretched leg and pulling

Fig 149

it back up, thus exposing the target. The victim prepares her legs and, as the attacker grabs her foot, she lifts her hips herself. *Note* the grip on the foot: the attacker's outside (L.) hand is on top of the victim's instep; his inside hand (R) is under her heel (*see* Fig 149).

Action: the attacker steps in on his L. foot and lightly snaps the R. foot (toes extended) in and out, the shoe-laces of his foot making contact with the curve of the victim's U.S. buttock, also making the knap.

In reaction, the victim will curl up, drawing her legs in and rolling to her side. The attacker's hands, in this grip, will easily release her foot.

A 'Good Kicking'

A 'frenzied' attack by a group of people or mob, will end up, when the victim has fallen to the floor, with the attackers using toe-caps, stamps and stomps to kick the victim to death. Theatrically, is quite difficult to make kicking a body when it is down look dramatically realistic. If the victim is surrounded by a number of attackers, many of the kicks can in fact be 'pulled'.

If these kicks are to make contact, then the 'top' of the foot is used, snapped in and out to a major muscle group on the victim. For example, the attacker's foot could make contact with the victim's stomach, or her cupped hand (*see* Fig 150).

If there is to be no contact, one 'old-fashioned' way of creating a dramatic effect is to used a toe-stamp in front of the target (*see* Fig 151).

Comedic Kicks

There are several types of 'comedy' kicks, including the bottom kick, the 'Charlie Chaplin' and the 'donkey' kick.

Fig 150

Fig 151

The Bottom Kick

This is a 'light' contact kick with the inside of the foot with a bent, turned-out leg – not with the toes up the coccyx (the partner's tailbone), as this is deeply painful!

Action: lift the knee, 'pushing' the instep of the foot against the victim's buttocks (*see* Fig 152).

An exaggerated reaction – perhaps a jump as the kick 'lifts' the victim off the ground – can give the impression of a 'chunky' kick.

The 'Charlie Chaplin'

In many of his films, Charlie Chaplin would be seen to sidle up beside the 'villain' and, from the knee, flick his boot out and up, striking with the outside of his boot the victim's bottom or, if the victim was taller (and they usually were), the top of their legs.

In reaction, the victim turns round to see who has just kicked him, but in the opposite direction to his assailant.

Fig 152

The 'Donkey' Kick

The attacker jumps up, flicking both feet together backwards to strike the victim's buttocks (the victim is usually bent over in some way – the more bent over, the greater the target). It is possible to make contact but, if the staging is just right and the reaction well timed, no contact is necessary.

A kick with one foot might disturb the composure of the victim, but a kick delivered with two feet should cause him to overbalance and then fall, roll, somersault – what he feels like. Enjoy it!

The Shin Kick

Whether using the toe, inside or outside of the foot, when performing a kick to the shin the attacker needs to use a 'stopping' kick. If light contact has to made, the victim should wear shin-pads.

In the English 'Olimpick Games', created by Robert Dover under the patronage of King James I around 1612, held in the Cotswolds and revived today, shin-kicking was a legitimate tactic within the wrestling contests. Further south, the Devonian style of wrestling was at one time principally characterized by kicking and tripping (as opposed to the Cornish style of 'hugging and heaving'). The extreme version was 'clogging', in the northern counties of England, which saw contestants wearing special hard-toed shoes to kick the shins of their opponent until he collapsed!

KNEE STRIKES

To the Face

At Right-Angles

For a knee (or upper-thigh) strike in the U.S./D.S. line, the victim prepares back and up.

Fig 153

Fig 154

The attacker grips the victim's head, and steps back with her 'kneeing' foot (*see* Fig 153).

Action: the two partners start the downward movement together, the attacker's hands slipping off so that there is no downward pressure on the victim's head. The victim bends his head down to the same height as the attacker's knee, but D.S. of it by at least 30cm (1ft) (*see* Fig 154).

The attacker carries her L. hand through to slap her U.S. thigh for the 'knap'. The victim reacts by lifting his head back up, his hands pushing off his thighs.

On the Diagonal

The knee strike to the face may also be performed facing the U.S. diagonal (this is my personal preference as a fight director).

The attacker prepares by bringing her R. leg back (*see* Fig 155) and adopting the same head grip as before, while the victim has his L. foot forward, ready for the reaction.

Action: as before, with the attacker slipping her hand of the victim's head to knap her rising R. thigh. The victim bends forwards, hands on his thighs, to the height of her knee (*see* Fig 156).

As the attacker walks through, the victim applies the 'billiard-ball' technique and, pushing off from his thighs, turns his face out towards the audience (*see* Fig 157).

Fig 155

Fig 156

To the Chest or High Stomach; Flank/Side; Groin

These strikes, which can be contact or non-contact, are not made with the bony knee itself but with the top of the thigh. As far as the audience is concerned, however, the energy and intention come from the knee itself.

To the Chest or High Stomach

This technique is a favourite in the film/TV fight repertoire (indeed, Captain Kirk seems to use it in almost every *Star Trek* episode or film).

Action: the attacker steps in from the side, grabs the victim by the shoulders, and 'pulls' him on to her lifting knee/thigh. The thigh

Fig 157

may appear to make contact, but it need not. It will depend on the victim's body type and on the staging.

Note: the attacker needs to be very careful not to actually pull the victim down on to her rising knee/thigh.

To the Side

As in Thai boxing, the attacker has to be in distance and supporting herself (*see* Fig 159).

Action: as she performs the action, the attacker needs to think 'up', not 'in'. The victim reacts by arching away from the strike, as if his lower ribs have been bashed in. This helps to give the illusion of contact, while minimizing any actual contact.

A forearm block may be added, but it is not necessary.

To the Groin

In fact, this is not a strike to the groin, but to the inner thigh. If contact is to be made, the partners need to be very close, with the attacker placing her hands on the victim's shoulders (*see* Fig 160).

Action: think of 'pushing' your hip towards the victim's inner thigh, making contact with the top of your thigh. *Safety note:* if you think 'knee', the knee will make contact, so don't!

The non-contact version of this technique is just as effective and a lot less stressful! In this case, the attacker simply lifts the knee centrally between the two partners; if she is wearing a skirt, the move will be even more convincing, as the fabric will keep moving, even when the knee has stopped.

In reaction, the victim will obviously experience a sharp contraction in the groin area, and his hands will go to the 'offended' part of the anatomy, drawing in the audience's focus. He should make an effort to keep his face up so the audience can see the 'pain'.

Fig 158

Fig 159

Fig 160

Sound: a strike to the 'soft' bits is difficult to 'knap', so a vocal reaction will be vital.

In theory, a hard strike to this area could cause sufficient pain for the victim to black out, so, like all groin attacks, it is not a technique that belongs at the start of the fight – unless the fight director wants it to end right there. In the film *Pale Rider*, Clint Eastwood uses a sledge-hammer, instead of his knee, to disable, most effectively, the baddy's henchman, played by Richard Kiel.

Fig 162

STEPS, STAMPS AND STOMPS

Step on to the Hand

This involves either 'light' contact or none at all. Theatrically, of course, there is no need for 'real' contact. This technique is also useful for treading on a wrist or hand to disarm a victim, and make him drop a gun or a knife.

Action: the attacker either places the ball of his foot on to the floor and, with his heel, 'grinds down' on to the victim's hand, or places his heel on the floor and puts 'pressure' on with the ball of his foot (*see* Fig 161).

Fig 161

Fig 163

Stamp on to the Foot

This is a non-contact move, delivered with a 'stamping' action – lift, stamp, lift. There are two methods. The attacker can stamp with the ball or heel of the foot to the floor (as above), and the other end 'stopping' over the target (*see* Fig 162). Alternatively, the whole foot can land flat on the floor, between the victim's foot and the audience.

A flat-footed stamp will create its own sound, and an additional vocal of 'shocked suprise' is always very effective.

In continuation, when using the second method, the attacker must bounce his foot back up immediately, or the 'miss' will be obvious to the audience. With the first method, it is less important.

The victim can react by lifting her foot and hopping around a little, followed by a bit of limping until the pain wears off.

Stomp to the Face/Throat

The aim is to stamp down and stay down on the target.

The attacker prepares by lifting his knee and placing his foot over the target, before 'driving' the stomp down. At this point the victim takes over control.

Action: the victim meets the attacker's foot with her hands and, holding it firmly, lowers his foot to her face, head or, more commonly, throat (*see* Fig 163).

The stomp can be carried through as a strangle. More likely, the victim will make an escape, by pushing or twisting and pushing off the attacker; 'giving' a little, breathing in, to cue the attacker. The attacker will bend his supporting leg and then use it to push himself off and away; if the action includes a twist before the push, he will turn himself. As the attacker falls away, the victim should extend her arms in a 't'ai-chi' push.

Safety note: the attacker must stay on balance throughout the technique.

Stomp to the Stomach or Back

This can be contact or non-contact. If contact is made, it must be very light – a mere 'butterfly kiss'.

In preparation, the higher the attacker lifts his knee before the stomp, the greater the audience's expectation. The attacker may also add a hop off the supporting leg for greater effect.

Action: stomp down, as above. However, this time there are no hands to catch the foot, so the attacker must immediately reverse the energy, 'pulling' the stomp and 'bouncing' off and away.

If you are using 'hop' as a preparation, time the stomp to arrive as your supporting foot hits, and so knap the floor. Vocals on the part of the victim can cover the moment of 'contact' (or non-contact). If the blow is to the stomach, the breath is driven from the body; if it is to the back, there will be deep pain!

In reaction, the victim arches his body up from the point of 'contact', whether front or back.

ROLLS

'A Contentious Man

If you have a Companion that disturbs your Mirth, and wou'd be rid of him, take hold of his collar behind, and with your Right put between his Legs as far as his Codpiss, and lift him up easily, and thrust him out of the Room, for he can never turn on you, but if you lift him too hard, you'l throw him on his Nose.'

(Sir Thomas Parkyns, 1713, publisher of *The Inn-Play or Cornish Hugg Wrestling*)

A roll is a movement that takes the body along over the surface of an object – the ground, a table, a partner's back. Conversely, a somersault 'rolls' through the air, not along a surface.

Protection

A roll is nothing to be scared of, but getting used to the floor does require practice. During the performance, you may do a roll only once, but in rehearsal you will do it over and over again, potentially leading to bruise upon bruise. Wear pads on your knees and elbows, and also on your back if you think you might get hurt. Knee and elbow pads are available from sports shops, while a pad for the back can be made from the modern camper's ground padding. There are also several types of back pad available that are designed for the equestrian sport of eventing.

No one is expecting you to roll around on concrete – yet – but even a wooden rehearsal floor might cause bruises and abrasions. Do not take chances. Use mats – gym mats for preference, or a mattress, or even a padded carpet. (You can also use martial arts mats, but they are only a step up from the floor.)

Gymnastic Forward Roll

The forward roll involves rolling from two feet on to two hands and then back on to two feet. Imagine that you have a ball held against your

Fig 165

Fig 166

Fig 164

Fig 167

stomach and curve over it; think about the ball rolling smoothly along a surface.

For a gymnastic forward roll, the take-off position is with both feet comfortably (hip-width) apart, knees bent, body weight lowered near to the ground (*see* Fig 164). Place both hands on the floor, arms bent softly, and begin to tuck your head in – chin to chest – as if to look back where you came from. Maintaining that position, rock forwards and push off from your feet. Keep the ball shape. Land on your shoulders, not your head, and continue to roll down your spine until both feet arrive on the floor (*see* Figs 165 and 166).

Landings

The Gymnastic Landing
If you have enough momentum you will be able to stand upright after doing a roll without using your hands (try reaching forwards).

Safety note: it is possible to bang your nose, if you tuck in too tightly, the roll is too violent, or your knees are tightly together when you arrive. Keeping the knees apart also creates a more stable landing base.

The 'Telemark' Landing
The landing position is reminiscent of a Nordic ski-jumper, and works particularly well when rolling off things, for example, a table. The forward momentum is taken up by landing first on one foot then the other (*see* Fig 167).

Improving Technique
As you grow in confidence, you can stretch out your legs as you take off. Next, try dive-rolling over a friend who is kneeling sideways. You will need more momentum for this, so you should practise the aerial entry: from a run-up, leap off one or both feet and dive through the air. Straighten your legs behind you, to get through, or over, your obstacle. Tuck your head under, to curve your spine and, using

your arms to absorb the impact, lower youself smoothly on to your shoulders and into the roll.

Helpful hints:

* Remember that you are a ball not a brick!
* If you have done a big take-off, you may land on your back and 'wind' yourself. It takes a little while to adjust, to attune your body to do what you want it to.
* Keep your legs and feet tucked under you, to avoid them hitting the floor heavily, and to enable you to stand easily.

More Rolls

Fig 168

Fig 169

Fig 170

Fig 171

Fig 172

The Actor's Forward Roll

The actor's forward roll is akin to the shoulder roll from aikido or judo, but without the hand slapping the floor (a breakfall).

To prepare, start with the rolling leg and rolling arm forward (*see* Fig 168). Rock back on the supporting leg, lifting the 'rolling arm', breathe in, and then move into the action: the leading hand arcs down to the floor, as if to tuck under the opposite armpit (*see* Fig 169). The head leads the arm, tucking under, as if to look back where you came from.

The body, having pushed off the back leg, pivots over the leading leg, rolls down the outside of the leading arm, on to the shoulder (*see* Fig 170) and diagonally across the back, to the opposite hip and buttock, landing on the outside of the now-bent back leg and flat on the 'leading' foot (not the heel), in a 'figure 4' position (*see* Fig 171).

The momentum of the roll can bring you up on to one knee before standing (*see* Fig 172).

The Flop

The flop is used to heighten the reaction, as if you have been stunned or hurt your back. The roll ends with you lying full length on your back, arms above your head, and legs in the 'figure 4' position. In continuation, you can either push down with the top bent leg and arch your back (as if it has been hurt), or, from the arch, with arms extended above your head, you can roll over on to your front, ending up in the 'recovery' position.

The Backward Roll

This is, of course, a roll in the backward direction, but, whereas the gymnast's backward roll is directly over the head, the actor's version is over the shoulder and upper arm (*see* Fig 173).

From kneeling, the action is to sit back, turning the head to look over the shoulder to where your knees are going to land. Now, take both legs and hands over the same shoulder. Finally, use your hands to push you to your feet.

The Side or Barrell Roll

This is a natural safety roll, which is useful if, for example, you are bumped into or pushed over. It is also the foundation of the action of rolling over a bench, a table, a person's back, or even the bonnet of a car.

From the starting position (*see* Fig 174), sit back on your heel as you lower your elbow on to the mat by your knee (*see* Fig 175). Start to roll across your back, with your back flat on the mat. Slow the roll down by extending your legs (*see* Fig 176). Tuck your L. knee and L. elbow in line; the action of 'tucking' will speed the roll back up and leave your R. leg extended (*see* Fig 177). As you arrive on your L. knee, turn your L. hand over and, palm down, use it

Fig 173

Fig 174

95

Fig 175

Fig 177

Fig 176

to push yourself up into the finishing position (*see* Fig 178).

From standing, the roll can be 'entered' by jumping sideways into a squatting position (like a frog); place your hands on the floor and, lowering your backside, enter the sideways roll.

Helpful hints: if you lower your shoulders, rather than sitting back on your heels, you will

Fig 178

end up doing a shoulder roll. If you lower your backside, and not your shoulders at the same time, you will end up doing a bottom roll instead. All are, of course, acceptable, just different types of roll.

Bull Dogging

Have your partner kneel on their hands and knees, sideways on – if you are a R. side-roller, their head should be facing to your L. You are aiming to jump over their rear end not their head end.

Run up to your partner, place your hands on the top of their hips and jump over them. Land and continue into a sideways/barrel roll.

Make eye contact at three points: first, before you run up; second, as you land; and third, when you have finished the roll. Finish the roll in some sort of 'on guard' position facing your partner – even if you are still on your knees.

The complete action is as follows: the 'jumper' runs up and jumps over the 'kneeler'; the kneeler watches the jumper land and then the two roll over together, as if the jumper has pulled the kneeler over with him. The two partners finish facing each other 'on guard'.

Rolling Over a Table

Standing
Stand sideways on to the table and hop on to it, positioning the knee and elbow as in Fig 175. (The hop is to prevent you smashing your R. hip into the table edge – pad the table with a mat as well.)

Barrel-roll over the centre and, as you come off the table, use your L. hand, if necessary, to steady you as you land (as in Fig 178).

From a Run-In
This roll might be used if, for example, a character is being thrown out of a bar or nightclub.

To do a R. roll: hop off your L. foot, quarter-turning to the L. in the air, land back on your L. and rock on to your R., hopping up into the roll as above.

PUSH AND PULL

In the opera, 'push and pull' refers to a performer being asked to move furniture on or off stage during a show, usually for a small extra fee. In stage fighting, the term refers to the techniques of 'pushing, shoving and barging', and to their counter action of 'pulling'.

Pushes

Hand Push
The cue for attacker and victim is the laying on of hands. In order to shift a taller or heavier

Fig 179

Fig 180

Fig 181

partner for 'real', the attacker will need to lower her centre of gravity below his. Theatrically, she will need to bend her knees.

Action: the attacker 'gives' a little, letting the victim lean in on her (*see* Fig 179), breathes in, then allows the victim to perform his reaction. Using his leading leg, he pushes himself off and away. The attacker then 'T'ai-Chi's her arms and body in the direction of the 'push' (*see* Fig 180).

Safety note: if the attacker really does push, using a force, energy and speed over which the victim has no control, the victim will go flying and there will be a significant chance of injury. The victim must always be in control of his 'exit'.

Push Away with the Foot
STANDING
The cue is the attacker placing her foot on the victim's thigh – not the knee joint (*see* Fig 181). The victim must make sure that he

presents a bent leg. In preparation, the attacker bends both legs.

Action: the attacker straightens out both the standing leg and the 'pushing' leg, and the victim reacts by stepping back as if he has been pushed.

LYING
The situation is that the victim is on the ground and, as the attacker approaches, he lifts one leg to keep her away. She then grabs his ankle as if to ward off the foot, but in reality she places it against her body (hip, stomach or chest). She then leans in, taking her own weight on her 'leading leg' (*see* Fig 182).

Action: the attacker pushes herself back off with her 'leading' leg. The victim straightens

Fig 182

the man may appear to have the dominant position, but it is in fact the woman, whose centre of gravity is lower than his, and who is behind him, who is in a position to collapse his front leg and either shoulder or hip barge him away.

Fig 183

his leg ('T'ai-Chi' style), giving the impression that he has 'pushed' her away.

Pull

The cue is the attacker grabbing the victim's arm. In preparation, the victim leans away, the attacker taking a step with him (*see* Fig 183). He takes a breath and then starts to run through past the attacker, as if pulled. As he passes, the attacker swivels her hips, leans into the 'push' and 'T'ai-Chi's her arms after him (*see* Fig 184).

USING THE SHOULDER AND HIP

Barges and Charges

When the two partners are positioned as for corps-à-corps in sword-fighting (*see* Fig 185),

Fig 184

Fig 185

Safety note: the two partners must be in contact before either one barges the other, otherwise the attacker may jolt his partner, causing a 'whiplash' injury.

Shoulder Barge

The attacker prepares by lowering his centre and, breathing in, 'giving' a little. His partner leans in and pushes herself off and away, using her legs. The attacker 'T'ai-Chi's the push with his body.

Hip Barge

In preparation, the attacker's hips need to withdraw a little from the victim, while the shoulders stay in contact.

Action: the attacker's body comes back in, as if to strike, and the victim's body 'bounces off', leaving the space. (Think of the 'perpetual motion' balls: one swings out, returns to strike the next ball, then stops dead as the other ball flies off.)

Note: the victim needs to have the legs bent so that he can push himself off and away.

Shoulder Charge or 'Tackle'

This can be done in a number of ways: from standing and lunging in; from a run; or from a leap in (creating a flying tackle).

The attacker should aim not to lead from the shoulder, which is bony, but instead endeavour to create a straight surface from neck to elbow (*see* Fig 186). On making contact, the attacker brings her free arm around to grab the victim's hip to steady herself.

The victim will probably need to take a step or more back to absorb the attacker's energy as she arrives – particularly if she is flying in. He should keep his hands up out of the way until contact, and then grab his partner to steady her, not allowing his face to smack down on to her back. (*See* also the Frontal Attack, page 58.)

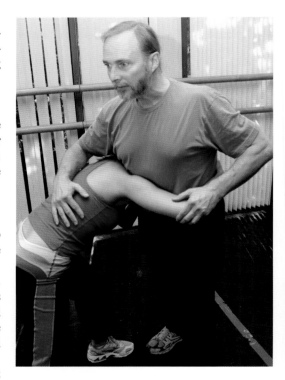

Fig 186

THE IRISH WHIP

The Irish whip is a wrestling technique in which the attacker whips the victim's arm up behind them, causing them to flip over forwards. Actors do not throw for real, obviously, and it is vital for the 'thrower' to let go so that the victim can control her own reaction (and before the victim's arm is wrenched out of its socket).

This technique is one of pure illusion and the audience's focus is deliberately split, with the thrower's energy apparently going in the opposite direction to the victim's.

In preparation, the victim stands facing down the mat. The thrower stands beside her and, using his dominant hand, takes the victim's R. wrist in a loose grip, lifting it up above her head. To keep her balance, the victim steps

Fig 188

Fig 187

Fig 189

back, leaving her 'rolling' leg in front (*see* Fig 187). The thrower adjusts his position, stepping sideways if necessary.

Note: there is a beat here – a breath – while the victim's body stops going backwards and prepares to go forwards. This is obvious to the victim; the thrower must allow for it and not start the throwing action too soon.

Action: the thrower begins the forward motion of the whip (unless it is to be totally victim-controlled, in which case she leads from the very first moment). Once past the vertical (12 o'clock), the thrower must let go of the victim's wrist (*see* Fig 188); she will need that arm to lead her into an actor's forward roll and if the thrower holds on to it, he will actually flip her over on to her back (this comes under the heading of 'advanced techniques').

In continuation, the thrower's hand continues to mirror the victim's until he starts to turn away (*see* Fig 189), to kneel on his inside knee, and the victim starts her roll.

The thrower now 'bowls a ball' (and scores a strike!), and the victim rolls. This is a perfect example of fight partners doing two separate physical jobs, synchronizing their actions to create an illusion.

HIP THROW

To carry out the cross-buttock hip throw, the attacker approaches from the side and, with his R. foot, steps across in front, angling his buttocks out across the victim's stomach/hips. His R. arm goes round behind her waist, while his L. takes hold of her R. wrist (*see* Fig 190).

At the second step, the attacker bends his knees and, pulling his L. hand down and leaning forwards, brings the victim up on to his hip. The victim does not jump up. The partners should be able to balance in this position quite easily (*see* Fig 191), then the attacker drives up with his legs, twisting his hips to the L., pulling

Fig 190

his R. arm, which is around the victim's waist, up and over his hip (*see* Fig 192).

The victim should fall over the attacker's hip to land, feet hip-width apart, in a kind of 'romantic kiss'/'tango-style' position. Then, as the victim swings over, the attacker bends his knees again, keeping his back straight, and lifts his L. hand up high, while supporting her with his R. arm (and R. knee), to keep her head and back off the floor (*see* Fig 193).

Fig 191

Fig 192

Fig 193

Fig 194

As the final step, the attacker lowers the victim to the ground, by one of two methods. In the first method, he releases his R. hand from around the victim's waist (she is still hanging on to his R. arm) and, bending his knees, he lowers her with his L. hand. Her L. hand, gripping, slides down his R. till her back touches the floor (*see* Figs 193 and 194). In the second method (which is preferable), as the victim falls towards the floor, the attacker makes a quarter-turn to his L., bends his inside (R.) knee (taking care not to bang it), and lowers her right down (keeping his back straight).

For a seemingly more 'realistic' landing, try a more vigorous throw – at first on to a crash-mat, at least 30cm (12in deep). The victim will probably land on her L. hip with the R. leg crossed over it, her L. hand most likely hitting the floor. She can extend her L. hand to 'break' her fall (*see* Fig 194). This 'breakfall' action also acts as a knap.

People in the stunt business say that, when performing any kind of falling stunt, the limbs should never land crossed, so as to avoid injury. Actors must therefore take care when doing martial arts-style breakfalls. Martial arts are just that – martial! Actors must be able to repeat the same move every night without fear of injury.

FAINTS AND FALLS

'In reality, trained actor-combatants don't fall at all, they simply re-distribute their weight gradually while moving from a standing to a prone position.'

Richard Lane, *Swashbuckling*

What happens physiologically, when a person faints, passes out, blacks out, keels over or swoons? Blood drains from the head, the victim becomes 'light-headed', darkness rushes in and, losing consciousness, the body collapses.

The body rarely falls unbendingly straight forwards, backwards or sideways; instead, it topples or collapses in on itself. Exceptions to this include soldiers passing out on parade – rigid at attention, they lose consciousness, faint and fall, still rigid – and the Hollywood masters of comedy – Charlie Chaplin, Buster Keaton, Harold Lloyd, and others – who always seemed to manage to fall over backwards, absolutely straight. (Of course, a number of tricks are employed to keep actors safe in film and television, many of which are not practical for an actor in the theatre.)

The techniques of 'falling' while standing on the floor will not necessarily be the same as those required when falling off something, or from a height, or down the stairs, nor indeed may they be sufficient.

Faints, side-falls and back-falls can easily be accomplished, once you have reached the knee. However, the action does not stop on the knee-cap; at speed, you will go down along the outside of your leg.

The Kneel-Twist-Sit

In preparation, the actor has her R. leg forward (*see* Fig 195) (having chosen the most comfortable).

Action: she starts to kneel, placing her R. knee about 30cm (a foot) in front of her L., counter-balancing with her arms (*see* Fig 196). Having completed the kneel, she now has a choice as to where she wants to end up: on her front, side or back.

For a side-fall, she swings her arms out to her R. (*see* Fig 197), sliding them along the floor, her body following, to end on her R. side, head cushioned on her outstretched R. arm, her L. in front, supporting her.

For a front-fall, as she swings her arms out to the R., she turns to face the floor. She

stretches out both arms, lands along the top of her R. thigh, and lowers herself down. Once down, she can 'relax'. You will be more comfortable with one leg on its side, the knee bent up forwards.

Note: avoid banging the knees.

For a back-fall from the kneel curl and 'sit' (legs in the 'figure 4' position), she lowers her chin to her chest, and uncurls down her spine (imagining unrolling a carpet) to lie on her back. The arms are carried through to rest above the head, not lifted and then dropped.

Try breathing out – sighing – as you fall, but do not relax the body while in motion.

Fig 195

Fig 196

Fig 197

Safety notes:

1. the head is heavy – you must not allow it to 'lead' the fall or it will make contact with the ground before anything else! It should be the last part of your body to touch the floor;
2. keep your muscles at least under minimum tension – nothing should flop or land heavily. Only once you are completely down on the floor may you relax your body.

The Step-Back-and-Sit

Step 1: Take a step back, keeping your weight on your front foot.

Step 2: Sit down on the heel of the back leg.

Step 3: Keeping your weight forwards (stretch out in front of you), sit back on the floor.

Step 4: Using the carpet analogy, unroll down your spine; your head is the last part to touch the floor – lightly.

Partners can assist each other in practising the transfer from standing to sitting (*see* Fig 198).

The Straight Back-Fall

Although the silent comedians of the early Hollywood movies did straight back-falls (or, at

Fig 198

least, appeared to do them), you should not try such a fall at home without a large mattress behind you. The stage actor's version may be a little different. Keeping your focus up and forward, take a small step behind you and, stretching out your other leg forwards, sit or fall. Once you are down, immediately stretch out your sitting leg. The idea is to mis-direct the focus of the audience up and away from your sit/fall technique.

Backward Trip or Fall

If you are pushed in the chest for real, your head will jerk forwards as your shoulders go back. In an attempt to regain balance, you will 'back-peddle' with your feet, probably flailing your arms. Should you now trip, your lower body will stop but your head will continue to go back. Bang!

In order to control this backward motion and sit/fall safely, you can bring your body back to centre by taking one or two controlled steps backwards to absorb the momentum. Now, 'contract' your stomach muscles – lean forwards – lower your chin on to your chest, and curl, lowering yourself to sit and, finally, roll back.

The Straight Fall-to-Prone

This is the fall experienced by the soldier who passes out (literally) on parade. The audience needs only to see you start (standing) and see you arrive (lying on the floor), not your journey.

There are a number of ways to progress from standing to lying:

1. crouch, bending your knees and taking your body weight as close to the ground as possible. Put your hands on the floor and 'walk' them forwards with cat-like tread until you arrive in the 'press-up' position, then lower yourself to the ground;

Fig 199

2. crouch, then swing your arms forwards, allowing your body to follow into the 'press-up' position, then lower yourself; this may cause a little shock to the wrists;
3. from standing, stretch out your arms and, leaning down and forwards, overbalance into the 'press-up' position; this will cause a little more weight and shock in the wrists and arms;
4. from standing, stretch out straight ahead of you and fall with your body straight; this will cause much more weight and shock on the wrists and arms;
5. from standing, with your hands by your sides and body straight, fall forwards, getting your hands to the floor just in time (*see* Fig 199; the hands have just started to move).

LIFTING, CARRYING AND DRAGGING

The Fireman's Lift
The 'lifter' prepares by taking hold of his subject's R. wrist with his L. hand, bends his knees, keeping his back straight, and puts his R. arm through her open legs, to grip her R. thigh (*see* Fig 200).

Action: the subject breathes in and, thinking 'up' (so there is no weight 'down' on to the lifter), she leans over into position. With his back straight and on balance, the lifter stands (*see* Fig 201). To put her down, he reverses his actions.

Moving a 'Dead Body'
The 'dead-body' lift may look good (*see* Fig 202), but it is hardly practical on stage. Faced with clearing a dead body from the scene, it may be preferable to grab both her legs and pull. Alternatively, it is possible to use just one leg (*see* Fig 203). Despite appearances, the subject has not relaxed but is maintaining a muscle tension throughout her body and, more importantly, keeping her head just off the floor, to avoid banging it.

Fig 200

Fig 201

Working in London's West End with Alan Ayckbourn on his play *Communicating Doors*, I was asked to help with (among other things) the dragging of a 'dead body' across the floor to the foot of some stairs. The two actresses could not move him, but a silver drinks tray placed under him meant that he slid easily along, as if on a sheet of ice.

exit, and the 'pullers' (all combat students) were positioned to ensure that his body and legs would clear the edge of the bar. It worked splendidly – and everyone had a go!

Fig 202

SLIDING

On the 2007 Summer School for NODA, one of the students, Gareth Hunter – or, to give him his 'fighting' alias, 'Tiny Toad' – expressed a desire to be thrown along and off a bar (*see* back cover picture).

When dragging, pulling or sliding a body, considerable friction is generated between the body and the surface on which it is moving. Sheets of paper were therefore placed under him to help him slide more easily. A few paper cups, which crush easily and safely, were added for effect. A large green crash-mat was placed at the end of the bar for his safety on

Fig 203

KNEELING

Do not allow any part of your body to strike the ground, making a 'clunk', particularly the 'sharp' bits – knees and elbows. Apart from possibly damaging the joint (which may never fully recover, especially if you 'thump' down every night on the same bit), it will affect the audience. Any 'natural' sound like this will jolt them back into 'reality', and they will begin to worry, not for the character but for you, the actor. The cast will have to work extra hard to get the audience back into the play.

Going down to your knees, you must always support your body weight. In one fight I choreographed, the actor's knees were so bad that, when he was shot, we had to have a piece of furniture strategically placed near by, so that he could grab on to it to lower himself to the ground!

Going to one knee, use the muscles in your legs to lower yourself under control, and protect your knees from a hard impact. You should make your landing on the floor as smooth and as gentle as the docking of the space shuttle!

Going to two knees, counter-balance by leaning back and let one knee arrive on the floor just ahead of the other.

3 WEAPONS

There are new laws regarding the use of all weapons in Britain and its theatres today and anyone intending to use weapons in any kind of show should read up on the situation first. The Violent Crime Reduction Act of 2006 concerns the serious tightening up of many aspects of 'real guns and real weapons', but there is provision within the Act covering weapons used in theatrical productions.

www.littletheatreguild.org
Grey Paper, no. 13, Nov 2007

At the time of writing, there is further information to be had in the HSE publication 'Management of firearms and other weapons in productions'.

INTRODUCTION

'Actors are the most dangerous people to have to duel with...because we don't know how to handle ourselves...We come out charging, whirling all around, forgetting the prepared routines of swordplay.'

(Errol Flynn, *My Wicked, Wicked Ways*)

The early Hollywood swordmasters, Henry Uyttenhove and Fred Cavens, were trained in

(Opposite) Girl with a sword: that's all you need!

military swordplay at the Belgian Military Academy. The next generation of both screen and stage swordmasters were trained in the sport of fencing, some to Olympic standard.

During the 1900s, sword-fighting in the movies went through several changes. The Hollywood swashbuckling era (from the 1920s to the 1950s) gave way in the 1970s to what an American described as the 'verismo' style, the style of William Hobbs, arguably one of the best contemporary fight directors. His 'realistic' style of swordplay, together with the 'acting' intentions that he gets from his actors, take his fights beyond the theatrical into the absolutely believable. *The Three Musketeers, The Four Musketeers, The Duellists, Cyrano de Bergerac* and *Rob Roy* are just a few of his films.

In 1987, Bob Anderson and Peter Diamond revived the Hollywood 'swashbuckling' style with the film *The Princess Bride*. Bob Anderson had, at one time, been a British Olympic fencing coach. Peter Diamond, an excellent British stunt co-ordinator, had also studied

Erich Wolfgang Korngold was one of the greatest composers for the 'swashbuckling movies' of the 1940s and 50s, including *Captain Blood, The Adventures of Robin Hood* (starring Errol Flynn, Olivia de Haviland and Basil Rathbone), *The Sea Hawk*, and many others. His epic scores beautifully encapsulated the spirit of these heroic, colourful, life-affirming films.

sport fencing. Between them they brought back the 'swish and ting' style of sword-fighting and, with it, the glamour, 'pithy' dialogue, music and sheer joy that exemplified the classic swashbuckling films.

Since the release of *The Princess Bride*, the 'swashbuckler' or 'romantic historical adventure' movie, has gone back and forth between the fighting styles of William Hobbs (as in *Rob Roy* with Liam Neeson), and Bob Anderson (who worked on *The Mark of Zorro*, with Antonio Banderas). Alongside them, moviegoers have had fantasy films, such as *Star Wars* (also Bob Anderson) and the Matrix series. The fighting styles in these films are not new but based on ancient oriental techniques. Japanese sword techniques are seen in the films of Akira Kurosawa, while Chinese-style kung-fu is associated with Bruce Lee, Jackie Chan and Jet Li. Chinese-style swordplay has enhanced films such as *Crouching Tiger, Hidden Dragon*, *House of Flying Daggers* and *Hero*; with them has come 'flying', which is now an essential ingredient in most fighting films, including *Kill Bill: Vol. I*, with its magnificently choreographed fights.

Meanwhile, increasing numbers of civilian practitioners are studying the history of warfare, then experimenting with the combat techniques. There are many societies who have no intention of putting their work on to a stage. They study for the pleasure of understanding the past and, physically re-interpreting the words and lessons of the ancient masters.

Warning: the techniques found in historical manuals are for real combat, for example, duelling. If they are to be used for stage fighting, they must be carefully adapted.

CRUNCH OR POKE

Dawn, the beginning of time. An ape-like creature picks up a bone and, 'crunch', in slow motion he uses it to smash to pieces the skeleton of an animal (*see* the film *2001*).

The basic 'poke' principle of sword fighting is familiar to all. As Antonio Banderas, in the movie *The Mask of Zorro*, replies to Anthony Hopkins, when asked if he knows what he is doing with the sword, 'Yes. The pointy end goes in the other person.'

The principles of armed combat go as follows: develop a crunch; develop protection while crunching back; develop a poke to get inside the protection while dodging the crunch, and so on, and so forth.

A classical sport fencer wins his bout by scoring more points than his opponent, either by the 'poke' or 'crunch' method. He scores a hit by driving the point (foil or epée) or the edge (sabre) on to the body of his opponent with sufficient force to penetrate it – if they were not wearing the special jacket and

I saw an amazing production of *Hamlet* in Hamburg a few years back. During four hours of Shakespeare in German, the only words I understood were '*Sein oder nicht sein*', but I understood everything that happened on stage because it was told in such a spectacular fashion. The fight was choreographed by Malcolm Ranson, one of the current top British fight directors. Shakespeare set the fight as a fencing match, so in this production it began in the modern sport fencing way, with masks and jackets. The fight progresses, Hamlet does well, scoring a couple of points, and Laertes, frustrated that he cannot hit Hamlet (and driven by inner demons), 'fouls' and spikes Hamlet with his now buttonless and poison-tipped sword. The fight rapidly disintegrates into a brawl, the masks are lost and the careful, almost elegant, epée contest turns into an ugly bloody mess as the fighters struggle for survival, until claimed by death.

mask designed to prevent that occurrence. On stage, unless it is a particular choice, the actors will not be wearing masks and, more importantly, they should not be hitting each other!

Theatrical fighting with weapons is like dancing with attitude. The two partners weave a pattern of movements with physical and acting intentions in order to tell a story. The members of the audience are mesmerised by the magic of the story-telling and will, for that moment, suspend their common sense to believe in the fight, and the woundings or kill that follows.

In practical terms, if you do not have the freedom to spike your opponent with the tip nor cut them with the edge, you need to learn how to create the illusion.

Some Basics

There are a number of basics that need to become second nature.

Holding the Sword

For the rapier (*see* Fig 231, page 134) and for the smallsword, the two most common positions are the following:

* palm up (as if you are holding a plate of soup in your open hand); lightly close your hand, so that you see your fingernails (fingernails up, or 'supination'; remember it by thinking '*soup*ination'); or
* palm down, so that when you lightly close your hand, you see your knuckles (knuckles up, or pronation).

The third, and most natural, hand position is the relaxed open-hand position, as if preparing to shake someone's hand, hold a sabre (*see* Fig 204) or pistol or even a tennis racket (used for the broadsword and the dagger).

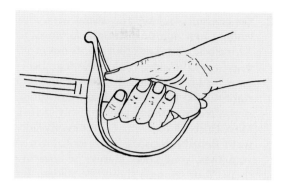

Fig 204 The 'sabre' grip.

On Guard

Once the sword is in your hand, you need to know how to stand with it, ready to fight. This position is referred to as being 'on guard'. Simply, it is a starting position from which you can either launch an attack or begin to defend yourself.

Brian Pitman describes this beautifully in his book *Fencing: Techniques of Foil, Epée and Sabre*; according to him, it is not only a physical position but also 'an attitude of mind'. He draws a parallel with a 'workman who, when beginning a job, first rolls up his sleeves'.

There are basically two generic on-guard positions: the R. on-guard position (in which the leading foot is the R.); and the L. on-guard position (leading foot is the L.). The leading foot is the one on the same side as the hand that holds the sword.

There are a number of ways of getting on to the feet:

1. from a chair: sit on the edge with your legs comfortably apart, your feet naturally following the line of your knees. Leave the feet flat on the floor and stand up. Now, turning to face one side, adjust the 'leading' toes out a little, bend the knees, and you are in an on-guard position;

2. the conventional method: stand with your leading foot pointing straight forward, to 12 o'clock. Your back foot points out at 90 degrees to the side. With heels together – back heel beside the front heel – create a right-angled triangle. With the front foot, step directly forward about 35cm (14in). Move the back foot 5cm (2in) directly sideways. Bend both knees; if you look down at your toes, your knees should be covering them. Your triangle should be strong, yet elastic, with the weight evenly distributed so that you can move in any direction.

Notes: your legs must become like 'coiled springs' – strong and elastic – ready to move you in any direction, at any speed, at any moment; the actor in you should be aware that, if you bend your knees in this triangular stance, you will look good – as if you are ready to fight.

Body
With your front foot pointing straight ahead and your back foot directly out to the side, your body should naturally face into the diagonal.

Arms
In this position, curve the arms up above your

Fig 205

head, as if you are holding a beach ball. Now open them out to the side, still curved, with palms up, until they are roughly shoulder height.

To position the front or sword arm, drop your elbow until it is a hand's width from your waist (*see* Fig 205, front). The hand is in supination, and the arm can move freely sideways and can be pulled back as well as being extended forwards. For pronation, turn the hand over and lower it a couple of inches, as if placing it on a table in front of you (*see* Fig 205, rear). Your elbow will rotate out a little, which is fine.

The back arm has many positions depending on whether it is holding a defensive weapon – a shield or a cloak; a dagger; even a second sword. Empty, it can be used to deflect an attack, although its primary purpose is to counter-balance your movements.

Head
To quote Errol Flynn, 'Look forward, your head proud.' Condition your body to this 'on-guard' position, which must become second nature.

THE STUDY OF FOOTWORK

> 'Never put a sword into the hand of a man who can't dance.'

Unless you are going to fight sitting down, or standing in the rigging of some pirate vessel, or, perhaps, flying through the air, you need to be able to move your feet. The 'How To' dance manuals from the first half of the 1900s showed footprints and directional lines drawn on the floor to aid in the learning of the waltz, quickstep, cha-cha and other ballroom dances. In similar ways, many combat masters enabled their students to follow, quite literally, in their footsteps.

This book will use the floor compass, or clock-face, in order to give directions for the body or movement. The compass directions radiate clockwise or deosil (sunwards). You stand at its centre and it turns with you. (Using a touch of Middle Ages reasoning, imagine yourself being at the centre of the universe.)

To make it easier to follow, draw it on the floor (using chalk or tape). If you wish to simplify it, draw a simple 'cross' instead of the tramlines see Appendix Diagram 4.

North = Straight ahead or 'front' (12 o'clock)
North-east = Front right 45 degrees or diagonal Fwd R.
East = Side right 90 degrees (3 o'clock)
South-east = Back right 45 degrees or diagonal Back R.
South = Directly behind you or 'back'
South-west = Back left 45 degrees or diagonal Back L.
West = Side left 90 degrees (9 o'clock)
North-west = Front left 45 degrees or diagonal Fwd L.
And back to North = Straight ahead or 'front'.

This subject is covered in depth in an excellent study entitled *Of Paces: A Comprehensive System of Footwork for Stage Combat* by Payson Burt, a member of the Society of American Fight Directors.

Movement Through Footwork

In battle, the warriors charge at each other, the front lines crashing together in a heaving mass (perhaps it is only in films that they run through each other). There is very little organized 'footwork' involved. However, anyone fighting against a single opponent will need to have more control over the way in which he moves.

The walk, or the pass, is the simplest way of moving. Stand up and take one step forwards; you are ready to begin. Now, take a second step. Your back foot has just made a pass forwards. Begin on guard and finish on guard.

The Single Pass Forwards

From the R. on-guard position, knees bent, pass your left foot forwards to point to 12 o'clock, swivelling your R. (now the back) foot, to face Side R. 90 degrees, and resume 'sitting' (triangular stance). You are now in L. on guard.

Each time you do a single pass forwards you will need to swivel out the back foot.

The Single Pass Backwards

From the L. on-guard position, prepare to pass your L. (leading) foot back. Before you do so, try swivelling the R. heel back (swivelling the back heel first opens the hips, and this may help). Then pass the L. foot back, turning it out to face Side R. 90 degrees (triangular stance).

The Double Pass

The double pass involves two steps forwards or backwards. However, if you were to swivel the back foot each time you did the double pass, the movement would look very ungainly, as well as being slow.

Instead, leave the back foot facing sideways as you pass (like a ninja in the night), completing the double by bringing the second foot through into the on-guard position.

Passing backwards, there is no need to open the hips first. Simply pass the leading foot back as if walking, then bring the second foot, in its ninja position, back to the on-guard position.

Methods of Turning on the Spot (*see* Appendix Diagram 5)

Slip and Pivot

Position 1: on the edges of the top box, stand in R. on guard facing North, the toes of your R. foot touching (a), your L. foot toes touching (b).

Step 1: to slip, slide your L. foot back across the middle line until the heel touches the outside edge of the second box (c); the leg will now be almost straight.

Step 2: now pivot your body 180 degrees L. and you are in L. on guard facing the back wall.

Step 3: pass your R. foot forwards to (d) and you are ready to slip, pivot and pass forwards to return to the starting position.

Cross and Pivot

Stand in R. on guard facing front, as above, R. foot at (a) and L. foot at (b). Cross your R. foot to the L. edge of the top line (e) and now pivot to face the back wall.

To return, slip and pivot and you are back in R. on guard facing front (North).

Alternative Steps

Fighting involved more than just forward and backward movements – you might need to avoid an attack by skipping sideways, or on the diagonal, for example. You need to think also, for a moment, about your attack. Your opponent is armed with a sword and dagger. You are in civilian clothes and vulnerable to that sharply pointed and rather long rapier. Do you attack head-on? You might be better off going around the side, probably towards the shorter weapon. This may be a rather simplistic scenario, but the idea is there.

The Side-Step (see Appendix Diagram 6)

Position 1: stand with your feet parallel, hip-width apart, toes pointing forwards. Before you start to move, bend your knees. From this position, step a small pace to the R. (a to a1) and then follow it sideways with your L. foot (b to b1). Do not close the feet together, but finish as you began, hip-width apart.

Make the count 1 - 2, 1 - 2, 1 - 2. as you side-step R.- L., R. - L., R.- L.

Now step to the L. – the aim is to develop your co-ordination evenly. As you become comfortable, change the rhythm – pace it up

by bringing the back foot in faster. Instead of 1 - 2, make it 1- 'and' 2- 'and'.

Keep the knees bent!

The Crossing Step (see Appendix Diagram 7)

To visualize this, think of Zorba the Greek or the 'vine step' in line dancing. You will be travelling in a line sideways. Step with the R. foot (a to a1). Cross the L. behind it (b to b1) and continue – R. to the side, L. in front, R. to the side, L. behind, R. to the side – until you get the idea.

Patterns

Traverse, circular and linear (forwards and backwards on tram-lines) steps can all be done. Whichever way you go, echo or mirror your partner's steps and their direction of movement; as long as you match, you can mix.

To practise a stepping exercise, start with the side-step around the circle, then use the crossing step to traverse the space, before passing forwards and backwards in linear fashion on the tram-lines (*see* Appendix Diagram 8).

The demise of the 'passing' step was matched by the rise of the gentleman who fenced for exercise and fun. The on-guard position echoed the duelling stance of the day, not with swords, but with pistols, and with the feet at such an extreme angle, it was difficult to pass forwards or backwards. Instead, it was simpler just to step forwards, bringing up the back foot behind the front, and vice versa.

Stepping Forwards – The Advance

Starting from the on-guard position, lift the toe of the front foot and, with the heel grazing the ground, advance the front foot about a pace. Land through the heel.

Bring up the back foot, lifting it from the knee, still turned out to 90 degrees – over the ground, not dragging – and place it, maintaining distance. In this way, you will have advanced one pace.

To help you with the timing, imagine a piece of elastic tied between your ankles. When the front foot moves, stretching the elastic, the back foot is almost immediately pulled after it.

Stepping Backwards – The Retire
Lift the back foot off just above the ground, and push it back a good pace. The push comes from the front leg, through the heel. Peel up and off the front toe and bring the front foot back in, maintaining distance. You are once more 'on guard'.

To re-cap: going forwards, lead with front foot; going backwards, lead with the rear foot.

BASIC ATTACKS WITH THE POINT

The On-Guard Position
The sword is held at a 45-degree angle, the tip pointing towards your opponent's eyes. When you are about to attack, before you move the legs or body, you must lower the point of your sword and aim at the intended target. This is first a major safety issue and, second, it cues your partner as to where the attack will come.

Now, imagine a laser beam extending from the tip of your sword, in a straight line, to the target. When you extend, thrust or lunge, the tip of your weapon should follow the path of that beam.

The Extension
Once the point of your sword is on target, straighten your arm, extending the point towards that target.

If you are in supination, or 'fingernails up', imagine smoothly offering your partner a plate of jelly. If you jerk your thrust, you splurge it all over them and miss the target.

If you are in pronation, or 'knuckles up', make a smooth punching motion towards the target.

Safety note: keep the point down all the way in and out. Your partner does not want to see your point 'dolphin-ing' through his eye line.

The Thrust
The thrust is an extension 'with attitude'.

The Piston Thrust
Step 1: lower your sword-tip in line with the target (*see* Fig 206, right).
Step 2: prepare by pulling your elbow back, your wrist into your hip area (*see* Fig 206, left). (This is Position 1.)

Fig 206

Fig 207

Step 3: thrust the sword forwards, fully extending your arm (*see* Fig 207, rear).

Step 4: pull the sword back from the elbow and return to Position 1.

Safety note: holding your sword with your knuckles up helps keep the point down.

The Jab/Stab
With the point already aimed at the target, the jab/stab is a less smooth extension – a 'poke' fast in and fast out (probably more suited to knives than swords).

The Lunge

Performing the Lunge
From the full extension (*see* Fig 207, rear), kick out forwards with the front foot, simultaneously straightening the back leg, jamming the back foot flat on the floor (*see* Fig 207, front). Think of pressing the little toe back and down. The front foot travels half an inch over the ground, arriving through the heel; the knee bending until it is directly over the ankle.

For the final position of the back hand in the lunge, imagine you are on a swashbuckling adventure in a land full of giants and dwarves, and innocents to rescue. As you lunge in pronation, your back hand should arc back to land on top of the head of the companionable dwarf alongside you, giving you support and strength in your extended and vulnerable position. This may not be classical but it is theatrical! If you attack in supination (fingernails up), your back hand remains palm up, open to the sky. As my dear friend, Belgian swordmaster Jacques Cappelle, once said, 'The classical back-hand position should mirror the position of the sword hand.'

The back hand, meanwhile, has counter-balanced the forward momentum by travelling back and out in an arc, to end in line with the shoulders.

Helpful hints: the tip of the sword is the first thing to move forwards, the lunge carrying it down the laser beam on to the target – tip, arm, body in. It is last coming back out – body, arm, tip out.

Lunge check points:

* Sword arm straight to the tip of the sword.
* Front toe pointing straight forwards, to 12 o'clock.
* Front knee also pointing straight forwards and directly above the ankle.
* Back leg straight, with the back foot flat on the floor. Do not let it roll.
* Hips and shoulders facing the Front L. 45 degrees, not sideways.
* Back hand in line with the shoulders, to the Back L. 45 degrees.

Recovering from the Lunge
Simultaneously, push back off the front foot; scoop your back knee out and back; lift your back arm, curving it up with energy (grab the Dwarf's hat and throw it into the air) and, most importantly, 'sit'. It is much easier to recover to a standing position but as a fighter you are then vulnerable, so you need to sit and be a coiled spring ready to continue.

Finally, the sword comes back and you are once more on guard.

BASIC ATTACKS WITH THE EDGE

The 'true' edge is the side of the blade that you cut with; most swords have a knuckle-guard on that side to protect the hand. *See* the swept-hilt rapier in Fig 231, left (page 134); the 'true' edge is the R. edge of the blade and the 'false' edge is the L.

The cut can be delivered from the shoulder, the elbow or the wrist. The attack delivered from the wrist will be faster than that from the elbow, and the cut delivered from the elbow will be faster than that from the shoulder.

The more powerful the intended blow or the heavier the weapon used, the more the body needs to come into play delivering the cut. The leading leg also needs to be advanced forwards in support.

There are a number of possible targets:

* on to the head, delivered vertically;
* the biceps on the arms/the short-sleeve 'T'-shirt line, delivered horizontally;
* to the thighs, on a slight diagonal.

Fig 208

Cuts That Stop or Are 'Pulled'

Cut to the Head (see *Appendix Diagram 9*)

To perform a cut straight to the top of the forehead, start with your sword on your shoulder.

Extending your arm, punch your fist at the intended target. Squeezing the grip of the sword tightly, which tilts the wrist slightly forwards.

Safety note: you should finish a hand's-breadth off the target.

Helpful hints: if you squeeze the grip, you should not be able to over-extend your wrist into a straight line (which requires a loose grip) – *see* Fig 211, page 122.

The Molinello or Moulinet

Originally designed for cavalry, this strike involves circular movements made by the sword-wielder to either side – on the inside or the outside – of his horse or round above his own head.

Stand facing your opponent, leading leg forwards, with your sword pointing at them. Extend your sword forwards (R.-handers). With knuckles up, your point will be out to your L. (your partner's R.). With fingernails

up, your point will be out to your R. (your partner's L.).

Inside: from knuckles up, drop the point, turning your wrist and bending your elbow, so that the point circles down, through the 'wrist-watch' position (*see* Fig 208, right). Finally, with your thumb on the underside of the grip, circle forwards, continuing to cut to the target's head (as above).

Outside: from fingernails up, drop the point and bend your elbow, turning your wrist out (*see* Fig 208, left). With your thumb now facing the back (releasing the grip with the last three fingers helps but you must maintain a strong thumb and forefinger grip), and the hand just off your shoulder, continue to the cut (as above).

Cut to the Biceps

This is a horizontal cut, which goes from your shoulder to your partner's shoulder.

Forehand

Preparation: from the vertical (*see* Fig 209, right), drop the blade back, to beside the shoulder, thumb and back edge of the sword lying alongside your biceps, fingernails up (*see* Fig 209, left).

Using the same cutting principles as when cutting to the head, punch towards the target

Fig 209

Fig 210

and squeeze the grip, extending the point to end a hand's-breadth off the target (*see* Fig 210, left).

Backhand
Carrying on from the forehand into the backhand, lift the point up, pulling the sword back through the vertical on to the backhand side (*see* Fig 210, right). Continue to prepare for the cut by placing your thumb and the back edge of the blade against the biceps of your other shoulder, knuckles up, then cut, as above.

Cut to the Thighs
This cut is made on a slight diagonal.

You should use exactly the same principles as above, but the preparation position is from your hip area, extending the cut to your partner's upper thigh.

Cuts That Go Through

Diagonal Cuts
Give a stick to a boy and he will instinctively attack with diagonal swishing cuts. It is the most basic and natural of movements, particularly for the Japanese or Arab curved sword, which is designed to cut and slice.

For the *sweep cut*, make a good preparation up and back and then, leading with the point, 'sweep' the cut through the target. Let the weight of the blade do the work. This cut is used for slashing attacks.

For the *draw cut*, as the blade arrives at the target, stop the energy through the target and pull your sword hand back to your opposite hip, drawing the cut back, yet seemingly still through the target. This is effective against parries and for 'wounding' and 'kills'.

The Wheel-Cut Diagram

The wheel-cut diagram (*see* Appendix Diagram 10) is the most common of all 'cutting' diagrams and can be seen, with alterations and additions, in most books or on the wall of sword-fighting schools. Its use applies to weapons ranging from the broadsword to the British naval cutlass.

For a R.-hand dominant swordsman, a natural sequence is to start with number 1 and then keep the sword moving as you cut through from 2 to 7. From 6, drop the point and inside molinello up to 7, before cutting down to centre. At this point, you can add a thrust to centre if you choose (8).

You can, of course, alter the pattern of cuts – for example by cutting down (1), and then

120

immediately reversing the direction of the blade to cut back up (4). You would then swing the point around behind your head to cut down (2), reversing it to cut back up (3), now 6 to 5, before the outside molinello into cut 7.

TARGETING

Out of Distance but On-Target

A forward attack, with the point, is out of distance when, having finished going forwards, it has still not reached the intended target. Because there is air between the tip and the target, to maintain the illusion of an accurate attack, it must remain on target.

In Distance but Off-Target

An attack with the edge, from the side or above, should be made in distance, but it stops a hand's-breadth from its intended target (having been 'pulled'), and is therefore off target. To maintain the illusion of an accurate attack, there should be a hand's breadth of blade past the target when it stops.

An attack with the point can be made in distance but, to avoid hitting the victim, it is aimed off target during the attack.

AVOIDANCES

The first general rule of self-defence is 'Don't be there when the violence breaks out – be somewhere else.' However, the first rule of self-defence in stage-fighting is 'Remove the target. If it is not there, it cannot be hit.'

In the 'Safety in distance' diagram (*see* Appendix Diagram 11), the inner circle represents the attacker and the line, a weapon:

* 'a' is out of range and, therefore, in the safest area (unless, of course, it is in the pub next door);
* 'b' is right where the attacker wants you;

* 'c' is reasonably safe for the victim but only if the partners have been trained (advanced fighters only).

There are different ways of staying safe: 'a' maintains his safety by stepping back from the attack; 'b' applies avoidances such as leaning away, ducking or jumping (up and back).

Leaning Away on the Diagonals

An avoidance, to the R. or to the L, is in response to an attack on the diagonal, upwards or downwards. Try to lean the whole body away on the parallel diagonal, in a straight line from head to toe. The attacker does not have to be in distance to make this dramatically effective.

Ducks

Attacker: cut horizontally at your own shoulder height. Do not curve up or slice down.

Defender: (unless you are a dwarf fighting a giant, in which case it is hardly likely that you would need to duck), make sure that when you bend, you place one hand firmly on the floor, to ensure that you cannot rise or lift your head into the pathway of the attack; keep your eyes on the attacker; and watch the attack whistle safely over your head, rather than assume it has gone and stand up too early.

Jumping Up

While it is perhaps a bit of a cliché, leaping over a sword is great fun and still swashbucklingly effective.

In Distance

Make sure the attacker cuts under your feet. To get a good jump, the defender needs to prepare by bending his knees just as the attacker pulls his arm back in preparation to cut. Then he lifts his knees and feet up out of the way of the blade.

121

Out of Distance

Attacker: cut down towards, rather than under, the defender's feet. The defender still leaps, thereby maintaining the illusion.

Note: even if the jumper is above him, the attacker must not be tempted to cut higher than his partner's feet. The cut must still be made under them. The defender should still jump (from either a one- or two-foot take-off), but needs to be careful where he is going to and bend the knees on landing.

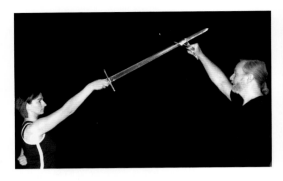

Fig 211

Jumping Back

Jumping back to avoid a cut with a sword or a knife, the defender bends his knees in preparation as the attacker gets ready to cut or slash. The most common jump-back is in response to a cut across the stomach, leaping off from both feet, pulling back away from the slash.

Safety note: as you go backwards, you will find your arms going forwards in counter-balance. Be extra careful that you do not leave your hands in the path of the slash. Consciously lift your forearms and hands out of range as you jump back.

PARRYING

The second rule of self-defence in stage-fighting is 'parry the attack'.

There are two basic forms of parry to defend against a partner's cuts and thrusts:

1. blocking parries stop the blade from entering your space. These parries meet the attack at right-angles (*see* Figs 211 and 212). One exception is the overhead sloping parry (*see* Fig 222, rear);
2. deflecting parries – placing your sword in a position that makes the partner's point attack glance by. These parries tend to work better held in a Fwd. 45-degree angle.

Fig 212

Whichever parry you use, all should end in a position away and outside your body, not directly beside or above it (facing your opponent, the line is the arm that holds your parrying weapon). *See* Appendix Diagram 12.

Historical weapon systems had any number of parries, with fanciful names in the language of their country of origin, for example, *porta di ferro larga* refers to an Italian broadsword parry. An all-purpose theatrical-parry numbering system is used today by most stage combat societies and academies. *See* Smallsword Parries, pages 144–146.

A Brief History of Weapons in Europe

Ancient warriors carried swords 'by right'. Knights on horseback carried swords; foot-soldiers carried swords, spears and bows; peasants carried farm implements. Knights, in their armour, could ride out accompanied by their foot-soldiers, bash a few peasants, and return to their castle of an evening for a bowl of soup and a haunch of venison. The peasants meanwhile did not fare so well.

However, during the 1300s, artillery was developed, followed by the musket and, eventually, any peasant could, without too much training and, from a safe distance, 'knock down' a knight!

In medieval times, fighting skills began to be worked on with some science. 'Fight manuscripts' began to appear in mainland Europe, full of illustrations showing the student how to use the sword, shield, dagger, and so on, but it was not until 1598 that a similar publication appeared in England. This was George Silver's *Paradoxes of Defence*.

Much of the foot-fighting of the time still relied on a certain acrobatic agility and in-distance techniques were vital to survival.

Fig 213

Fig 214

Talhoffer's *Fechtbuch*, 1467, contains a wealth of plates of in-distance fighting, and, apart from the obvious, such as wrestling and knife-work, swordplay also involved learning how to grab the opponent's blade or sword hand (*see* Fig 213); how to interlock arms or knees and wrestle; how to switch your own sword around and, grabbing the blade, use the cross-guard as an axe (*see* Fig 214); how to punch with the pommel (*see* Fig 217) (the action from which the term 'to pummel' derives).

In earlier times, the sword had been worn only by the soldier in battle, not in peacetime and not by a civilian. However, during the second half of the 1500s, the Elizabethan era, the young English nobility on the Grand Tour around the capitals of Europe would soak up the newest fashions – particularly those of costume, dance and swordplay – and bring their finds back to England.

One type of sword introduced from Spain and Italy was the rapier, a weapon worn by civilians. The blade was longer and thinner; the cross-guard had rings and bands added to protect the now-unarmoured hand; and the sharp point began to take precedence over the edge. Because the blade was 1.25m (4ft) or more in length, a defensive companion weapon – the dagger, a cloak, or a small hand shield or buckler – became necessary.

Conflict began to arise between the staid British sword and buckler play and the new fashionable Italianate rapier. It was played out not only in the streets of London, but also highlighted in the theatre. In Shakespeare's *Romeo and Juliet* the servants, Sampson and Gregory, carry swords and bucklers, while Mercutio, Tybalt and Benvolio, sons of the aristocracy, carry rapiers.

> In the narrow streets of London, the length of the sword (and the width of the Spanish ruff) became an issue. By the gates of the City of London, officials with yard-sticks measured the length of a man's sword and, if it was found to be over-long, it was cut down to size there and then.

In 1660, following the death of King Charles I, and the demise of Cromwell and the Commonwealth, the Monarchy was restored. Charles II returned from his exile on the continent, bringing with him all the latest French fashions, in clothes, music, dance and swordplay.

The Elizabethan Londoners had seen Italian masters teaching the rapier and now the Carolingian and Georgian Londoners were about to experience a French influence, with their new weapon, the smallsword.

As the smallsword and its techniques, which were still being usefully applied to duelling, reached the peak of perfection, the flintlock pistol made its appearance and very quickly becomes the favoured weapon to settle 'matters of honour'. (No particular training was required and smooth-bore pistols were not very accurate!) The civilian sword was soon

> At this time, in Europe, the dancing master was as likely to be a swordmaster as a teacher of style and court etiquette. In England, the teachers of swordplay were generally ex-military men, not well respected, and classed alongside vagabonds, prostitutes and actors.

relegated to the gentleman's club, and the skills once practised for the defence of personal honour become useful only for recreation. In the late 1800s, fencing began as a sport.

WEAPONS IN THEATRE

Ancient Greece

The Greek double-edged short-sword had a very distinctive leaf-shaped blade (*see* Fig 215); left, a reproduction of the sword Sting, from *The Lord of the Rings* film, designed after the Greek fashion. The swords are called short-swords because the blades were shorter than those of other swords; they should not be confused with the smallsword of the seventeenth and eighteenth centuries.

The shield is the Ancient Greek method of defence – as a Spartan mother would urge her son: 'Come back from battle with your shield or on it.' However, as Ewart Oakeshott writes in his book *The Archaeology of Weapons*, 'Not all the Greeks lived up to the harsh Spartan ideals.' The Ionian poet Archilochus was cheerful enough when he wrote:

'Some lucky Thracian has my noble shield;
I had to run: I lost it in a wood,
But I got clean away, thank God. So hang
The shield. I'll get another, just as good.'

Rome

The Roman soldier or legionary used a straight double-edged short-sword, the gladius. The blade was 50–60cm (20–24in) long and

Fig 215 (Left to right): reproduction of the sword Sting, from **Lord of the Rings***; nineteenth-century French Classical-style sword; reproduction sword of the common Roman soldier style.*

approximately 5cm (2in) wide. The grip was made of wood, it had very little in the way of hilt and the end of the sword tapered sharply to a point.

The sword in Fig 215 (right) is of the common Roman soldier style and was made by the props department of the BOVTS, for the play *Romans in Britain*. The blade is aluminium and slightly thicker than the original, as it was used for fighting. Its primary method of use was the thrust and cut.

The Roman soldier carried his shield in his left hand but, because the shield was large and quite cumbersome, he wore his sword on his right hip, suspended from a strap which hung over his left shoulder. All other right-handed

warriors throughout history wore their swords on their left side.

The 'replica' Roman swords available for hire from many theatrical armourers have in fact been made in the Roman style that was copied for the Emperor Napoleon (who loved the Classical style), and was carried by French soldiers in the late 1700s and early 1800s. *See* Fig 215, centre; this sword dates from the 1800s.

The Roman foot-soldier was taught to fight in formation and, with his sword, to thrust out from behind his shield, or *scutum*. He was also armed with a dagger and spears such as the *pilum*, a light, well-balanced throwing spear of about 1.8m (6ft), the top 60cm (2ft) of which were made of a 'soft' iron, which would bend on impact, rendering it useless to the enemy.

On the stage, such weapons are likely to feature in Shakespeare's history plays, and more up-to-date works such as *The Romans in Britain* by Howard Brenton. See also *Spartacus* with Kirk Douglas, and *Troy* with Brad Pitt and Eric Bana, among others.

BROADSWORD

'Broadsword' is a general term for all broad-bladed swords used during the period when Britain was invaded by the Vikings, the Romans, the Anglo Saxons and the Normans. However, broad-bladed swords continued to be carried into war by infantry until the advent of the musket.

When the Romans left Britain, in around AD412, they seemed to take with them the 'thrust'. The British continued simply 'cutting' or 'bashing', which led to the gradual development of armour until, by the 1400s, the knight was completely encased in plate armour (making him 'tinned food for dragons!') It soon became necessary to find a 'can-opener', and so the use of the sword changed its emphasis to thrusting rather than

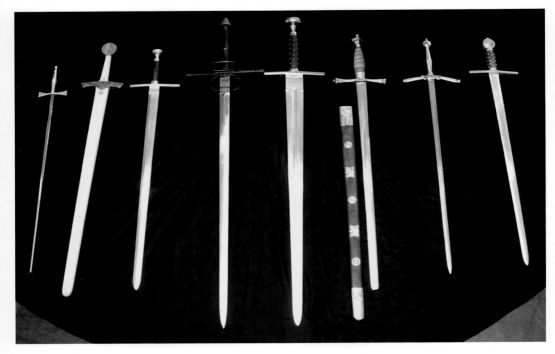

Fig 216 (Left to right): a Masonic sword; a wooden waster; an Alan Meek single-hand with aluminium blade; a John Barnett sixteenth-century 'bastard' hand-and-a-half in steel; an Alan Meek 'great' single-hand with Ali blade; a single-hand German steel blade and decorated scabbard; a slim single-hand steel; an Alan Meek single-hand with Ali blade 'after the film Narnia'.

cutting. A cut might glance off but a well-placed thrust would penetrate the little gaps that even the best-designed plate armour could not cover.

According to R.E. Oakeshott in his book *A Knight and His Sword*, 'a style of sword was designed which was simply perfect for a cut-and-thrust type of fighting – sharply pointed, with a broad blade stiffened by a ridge running down the middle from hilt to point'. These swords were generally light – on average a little less than 1kg (2½lb) – and beautifully balanced.

The generic theatrical single-hand broadsword would have an overall length of 82–80cm (33–36in), and a blade made of steel or aluminium. A shorter blade, of around 70cm (28in), makes for a lighter sword, which might be preferable. The wooden grip is bound with leather and the simple cross-guard made of steel or brass. There is a point of balance on the blade a couple of centimetres (about an inch) below the cross-guard.

Types of Broadsword

Wooden Waster
A light wooden replica sword, single or two-hand, much used for training by historical fight groups.

126

Hand-and-a-Half Sword
Also known as the bastard, this had a blade not much longer than that on a single-hand sword. The grip, with pommel, was just long enough for two hands when needed (*see* Fig 217).

Two-Hand Sword
A sword with a handle long enough for a soldier to grip comfortably with two hands; the weapon of a foot-soldier. The Scottish version (*see* Fig 219), the *claidheamh mor*, or 'claymore', was unique, with its downward-sloping cross-guards ending in 'quatrefoil terminals'.

Fig 217

The typical *zwei-hander* (Fig 217, left) has a wavy-edged blade. The combatant's left hand grips the leather-bound Ricasso, protected by small half-moon guards, or *Parrier-hakken*. A soldier might use this, the favoured weapon of German mercenaries, or *Landsknechten*, during the late 1400s to early 1500s, as a spear for thrusting or a pike for holding off cavalry.

How to Wear the Broadsword
Theatrically, with or without scabbard, the broadsword is carried in a frog (*see* Fig 267,

page 170), either hanging straight down by your side (the green one) or at a slight angle (the red one), or thrust through a loop of leather, a metal ring or a belt. Historically, it was hung from a belt with straps or chains (*see* Fig 218).

Two-hand swords were, in the main, carried over the shoulder, without scabbards. Sometimes they were strapped across the back.

Fig 218 Wearing the broadsword.

127

How to Hold the Broadsword

Single-hand: most broad-bladed swords have a cross-guard of some kind. With your dominant hand, hold the grip of the sword, blade point up, as you would hold a stick, golf club or tennis racket – the shaft rising in the 'V' between your thumb and forefinger. Make sure one of the bars of the cross-guard points towards you along your forearm; the other points directly away.

Two-hand: your second hand will take hold in a similar manner but below the first, as far down the grip as possible. Actually placing it on the pommel will give you more control and flexibility in action, particularly with the longer or heavier swords.

On Guard with the Broadsword

The historical manuals that deal with the broadsword, particularly Talhoffer's *Fechtbuch*, will give you some ideas about ways in which to adopt the on-guard position. Fig 219 shows a reconstruction of two of the two-hand on-guard positions.

How to Use the Broadsword

For revision, see the section on 'Basics Attacks with the Edge', page 118.

Horizontal Cuts and Their Parries

The forehand cut is done with the fingernails up. The backhand cut is done with the knuckles up.

Fig 220

Fig 219

Fig 221

Fig 222

The targets are as follows:

1. the head – towards the top of the forehead rather than straight down on to the crown;
2. the shoulders – actually to the biceps area or the line of the short-sleeve T-shirt;
3. the thighs – above the knees, at the mid-thigh.

Begin in an on-guard position (*see* Fig 223), points angled up; tips crossing by 7 or 8cm (3in) and touching, each to your R. side.

Fig 223

In the high line (*see* Fig 220), the swordsperson on the left demonstrates a single-hand parry of 3; the swordsperson on the right shows a two-hand parry of 4.

In the low line (*see* Fig 221), she demonstrates a parry of 2 (left); he shows a two-hand parry of 7, the 'leading' hand with fingernails up (right).

Vertical/Diagonal Cuts and Their Parries
Vertical or diagonal cuts can be made directly to the head, or from an inside or outside molinello (*see* page 119).

The overhead parries shown in Fig 222 are a parry of 5 (front), and a two-hand sloping parry of 5A (rear).

THE FIVES

This training exercise can be done with a single-hand or a two-hand sword and consists of five cuts. It starts with a cut to the head, followed by a cut to each shoulder, and then a cut to each leg.

The Stationary Attack (No Feet)
Step 1: the attacker begins the cut to the head with an outside molinello. As the attacker circles her blade past his L. side, the defender drops the point of his sword and lifts it overhead to parry of 5 (*see* Fig 222). The attacker now has a choice of targets: either a forehand attack to her partner's L. biceps or a backhand attack to his R. biceps.

Step 2: going into the backhand attack, the attacker 'bounces off' or 'pulls' the cut back off the defender's head, arc-ing down past his L. biceps, and extends her arm to cut to her opponent's R. biceps. The defender drops his hand

129

Fig 224

Fig 225

Fig 226

to waist height and parries High R. of 3 (*see* Fig 220, left).

Step 3: the attacker 'bounces' the cut back off, circles the tip of her sword around her head, down past her R. biceps, and extends her arm to cut to her opponent. The defender turns his body to face L., bringing his sword across to parry High L.of 4 (*see* Fig 225).

Step 4: the attacker 'bounces' the cut back off, the point up and around, lowering the blade to the area of her L. waist, and extends the cut to his R. thigh. The defender drops his point in a half-circle, turning his body R. and parries Low R. of 2 (*see* Fig 226).

Step 5: the attacker 'bounces' the cut back off, the point up and around, lowering the blade to the area of her R. waist, and extend the cut to his L. thigh. The defender can simply turn his wrists so that the edge of the blade faces L. and bring the sword across into a Low L. parry of 7. However, he could get more power into the parry and make it look much better, if he were to 'bounce off' from Low R., circle the tip of his sword up and around between you, exactly as the attacker, and, turning his body, parry Low L. of 7 (*see* Fig 221).

Step 6: to start the 'Fives' again, the partners can either return to the on-guard position, but with their blades now to the L. of each other, or the defender can take his turn, cutting to his partner's head from an outside molinello.

Parry angles: all the high cuts are parried with a straight sword, at 90 degrees to the attacking blade; all low cuts are parried at 45 degrees (the angle of the leading leg), except for parry 1, which is hanging straight down, at 90 degrees.

Travelling

In this version, the attacks are done with each partner advancing and retreating one step per cut. A cut to the R. side will be supported by a step forwards on the R. leg, and similarly to the L.

The attacker starts with the R. leg back, twirls an outside molinello, and then passes forwards with the R. foot as she cuts to the defender's head. The defender passes back, mirroring the attacker's advance. You should find that parrying to the L., your L. foot is back (opening your body to strengthen the parry); it is similar when parrying to the R.

This type of attack and defence features in Shakespeare's history plays, and films such as *Excalibur, First Knight, Monty Python and the Holy Grail* and *Braveheart*.

Companion Weapons to the Broadsword

The Buckler
With its centre-back hand grip, the buckler was not much bigger in width than a large plate, round or rectangular and wavy. The front could be plain or it could have a central boss, which sometimes stretched out in a sharp point.

Thirteenth-century manuscript I.33 has illustrations showing a pair of unarmoured

Fig 228

fighters, seemingly monks, in a variety of fighting positions. A couple of these stances are interpreted here. In Fig 227, the fighter on the left is in a 'defensive' pose, in which the sword is often positioned under the buckler arm instead; her partner is in an 'offensive' guard.

In Fig 228, the two partners are in a corps-à-corps (body to body), where, having parried an attack with his buckler, the right-hand fighter voltes round, bringing his sword arm up and over, trapping his partner's arms and her weapons.

Daggers
The dagger is an additional side arm that became a regular piece of equipment for both the military and the civilian. Some examples include the rondel dagger, so called because of

Fig 227

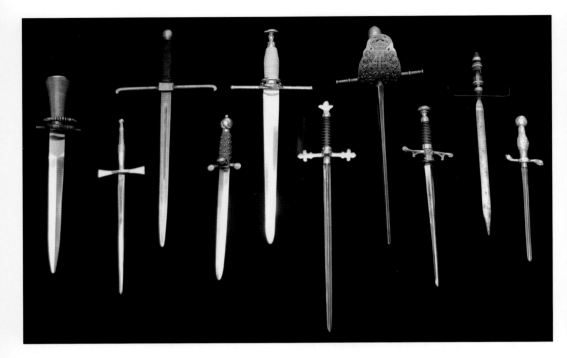

Fig 229 Companion weapons to the broadsword and rapier.

the round protective discs at either end of the grip; the ballock dagger, which has a simple wood handle with two 'globular' thickenings as the guard and a thin blade of 22–23cm (about 9in), tapering to a point; and the misericorde, which is similar in general blade shape, and sometimes triangular.

All these types of dagger were used for in-distance fighting – stabbing through chinks in armour or the eye-slots in helmets. They were also used for putting wounded or captured soldiers 'out of their misery'.

OTHER WEAPONS

There are a number of other weapons that used their weight, combined with the force with which they could be wielded, to crush or break through plate armour.

The Axe

Knights wielded single-hand axes. Previously, two-hand axes were wielded by house-carls, the elite bodyguard to King Harold in the mid-1000s. The Vikings carried short-handled axes for throwing.

The Hammer

A war-hammer was a heavy head of metal set on the end of a staff of perhaps 1.25m (4ft). On one side was the hammer, on the other, a spike or axe blade. It was usually a weapon for two hands.

The Mace

The mace, and similar weapons known as the 'morning star' and the 'holy water sprinkler', was a single-hand style of metal club with a wooden haft.

The Ball and Chain

Derived from a farmer's flail, this weapon was a short club with a ball of metal attached to it by a chain.

RAPIER AND DAGGER

Rapier

A rapier is a double-edged sword with an acute point and an elaborate guard for the hand. The guards were usually made of steel, but sometimes they were in gold or silver, in keeping, according to the New York Metropolitan Museum of Art, 'with the decorative embroidery and patterning of the masculine costume of the period'.

Some daggers were also exotic in design – the blade might be a scissors-type arrangement or have notched edges, like a comb, so that it could trap the rapier blade and, twisting, break it.

Types of Rapier Hilt
The 'swept' hilt was so called because of the elaborate interlocking of the rings of its guards.

The 'cup' hilt was identified by its obvious cup shape. It became synonymous with the swashbuckling movies made by Hollywood in the 1940s and 50s.

Types of Rapier Blade
The types of blade range from flat, via

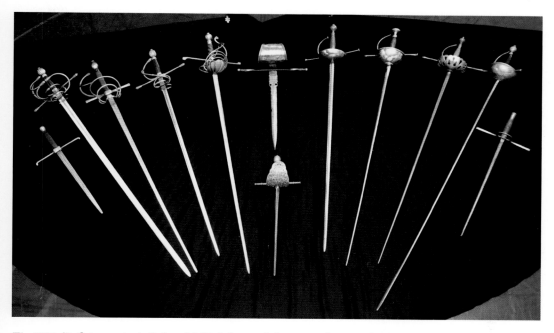

Fig 230 (Left to centre): Brian McKnight steel dagger; Alan Meek aluminium blade of 36½in; Brian McKnight steel 'fighting tool' (his words); Alan Meek steel; 'heavy' steel rapier, armouronline.com. (Centre): main gauche daggers – steel Victorian replica; Alan Meek, epée blade. (Centre to right): 1940s Robert White & Son Theatrical all steel; Alan Meek, brass cup with epée blade; Del Tin Italian steel with epée blade; brass cup with full-length diamond-shaped blade; Wilkinson 1898 practice steel dagger.

diamond, to triangular. Most theatre cup-hilt rapiers and smallswords today use the epée blade, a sport fencing blade, but there has also been a resurgence of 'flat' (Schlager) blades.

Because of its length, the rapier is more suited to the thrust rather than the cut, and it is therefore associated with a revival in the use of the point, leading to the thrust and lunge.

Holding the Rapier and Dagger

The swept-hilt rapier can be held in pronation (knuckles up); the cup-hilt version in supination (fingernails up) (*see* Fig 231).

The dagger can be held as in Fig 234 (left); with the thumb extended along the grip to the cross-guard (sabre grip); or, if the blade is wide at the base, with the thumb placed on its base.

Safety note: any finger that goes beyond the protection of the cross-guard is in danger of being cut!

Wearing the Rapier and Dagger

The rapier, worn in a scabbard, is slung low in a 'frog and belt' from the left hip.

The dagger can be worn behind the back, its hilt facing left for a left-handed draw. It was occasionally worn on the same side as the sword.

I found a Victorian replica of a 'main gauche' or left-hand dagger (*see* top centre in Fig 230) in an antiques shop. I asked the owner about the origin of the name. According to him, it was a Spanish-style dagger, and, while he was unsure about the 'gauche' reference, holding it up sideways, he explained that 'main' derived from the shape of the curved knuckle-guard, which was exactly the same shape as the sails on the galleons that plied the Spanish Main. I was enchanted by his explanation, and had to buy the dagger.

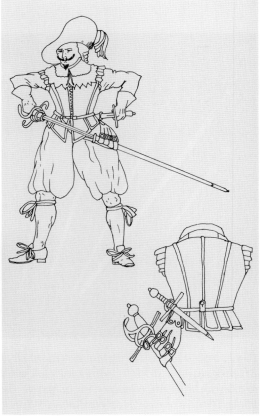

Fig 231

Fig 232 Wearing the rapier and dagger.

Basic Guards

In the defensive L. on-guard position (Fig 233, left), the dagger is comfortably forwards – the point need not necessarily be up – and the sword is held back in the R. hip area.

In the offensive R. on-guard position (Fig 233, right), the sword is comfortably forwards, knuckles up, and the dagger is back in the L. hip area.

When choreographing guards for fights, it is vital to research the period by referring to books or websites. In Fig 234, the partners are in 'guards after Thibault and Fabris/di Grassi'.

Fig 233

Fig 234

Basic Principles of Using the Rapier and Dagger

* Footwork: passing steps, single and double; side-steps; advancing and retiring.
* Primary functions: attack with the sword and defend with the dagger (the dagger parries and numbers are the same as for the sword, but reversed). As you become more used to wielding two weapons of unequal length, you can vary their use, for example, attacking with the dagger.
* For the following simple exercises: A = the initial attacker; B = defender. Attacks: out of distance/on target. Stance: both stand in offensive R. on-guard position. Distance: when the swords are extended the tips should remain apart the width of a splayed hand, tip of the thumb to the tip of the little finger.

Basic Exercises

Low-Line Sword Thrust – Dagger Parry 2
A: extend your sword to B's stomach.
B: half-circle your dagger down to catch the blade and remove it sideways to a position outside your body, Low L. (dagger parry 2).
Both return to on guard, A's sword withdrawing after the parry.
B: now extend your sword to A's stomach.
A: dagger parry of 2.
Both return to on guard, B's sword withdrawing after the parry.
Note 1: do not scoop the parry back up but leave it in position.
Note 2: when parried, the attacker must 'give grace'; allow your blade to be parried, 'giving' with a straight arm, not bending from the wrist.

Low-Line Sword Thrust – Dagger Parry 1
A: extend to B's stomach again.
B: drop your dagger point, turn your L. wrist (as if looking at your watch) and

135

push the dagger across to Low R. (dagger parry 1).

Return to on guard, before B repeats the attack for A to parry.

Helpful hints: you will have to raise your sword arm to get the dagger outside your body Low R.

High-Line Sword Thrust – Dagger Parry 3

A: extend to the centre of B's chest (no higher).

B: half-circle your dagger up inside to catch A's blade and remove it sideways to a position outside your arm, High L. (dagger parry 3).

Return to on guard before B repeats the attack for A to parry.

Note: Fig 235 shows a Capo Ferro 1600s pose, with the left-hand partner doing a dagger parry of 3. It is actually a R.-hand dagger parry, historically quite unusual and aimed at the target of the time – the face. This is not a move for the modern-day actor to attempt!

High-Line Sword Attacks – Dagger Parry 4

A: extend to the centre of B's chest (no higher).

B: holding your dagger with the point up, push it across your body taking A's blade to a position outside your body, High R. (dagger parry 4) (*see* Fig 235, right).

Return to on guard, before B repeats the attack for A to parry.

Fig 235

Helpful hints: in the high line you may have to lower your sword arm to get the dagger outside your body High R. while, in the low line you may have to raise your sword arm.

Attack on to the Head – Dagger Parry 5/5A

The stance is the same but the distance between the two partners is less – the point is just a couple of centimetres (almost an inch) off the chest.

A: make a molinello before attacking with the true edge to the centre of B's head.

B: as A's blade circles back away from you, start to bring your dagger up to a position Front High Fwd. 45 degrees (dagger parry 5/5A).

Return to on guard, before B repeats the attack for A to parry.

Safety note: A must first lift the point of his sword up and away off B's dagger before returning to the on-guard position.

Adding the Feet

The Lunge

Extend and lunge with each attack. Defender: if the point is coming too close, take a step or pass back before you parry.

The Passing Lunge

Distance: standing feet together, extend both weapons – the tips of the swords should touch the cross-guards of the daggers.

Stance: now both partners step back with their R. feet into defensive guards.

A: extend your sword to the target, then pass your R. foot forwards into a lunge.

B: pass your L. back, at the same time as A passes forwards, and then add the parry.

The Riposte

The riposte is the defender's reply. In the basic

exercises, once you have completed the first two moves – the attack and the parry – the defender ('B') is in a position to riposte or 'attack back in time':

B: (holding the parry, so trapping A's sword) with no footwork, extend your sword towards A's inside thigh.

A: (holding your sword still extended) with no footwork, half-circle your dagger down (dagger parry of 2).

Start the exercises in the low line and, when both of you are comfortable, change the riposte into the high line, with the dagger parry of 3.

Saviolo's Circle

This is a method of practising the low- and high-line parries, 2 and 3, against piston thrusts. Steps used are the side-step, progressing to the side crossing.

The Side-Step

Start facing each other, your weapons held as if on a table in front of you ('ready') and feet hip-width apart. Step out together, in a circular path, right feet first, then bringing in the left, maintaining distance ('close').

Attack and parry: two attacks to the stomach, two attacks to the chest.

In the low line:

Step 1: on the R. feet, A thrusts stomach. B does a dagger parry of 2, Low L.
Close 2: the L. feet, weapons 'ready'.
Step 3: on the R. feet: B thrusts stomach; A does dagger parry of 2, Low L.
Close 4: the L. feet, weapons 'ready'.

In the high line:

Step 5: on the R. feet, A thrusts chest. B does dagger parry of 3, High L.

Close 6: the L. feet, weapons 'ready'.
Step 7: on the R. feet, B thrusts chest. A does dagger parry of 3, High L.
Close 8: the L. feet, weapons 'ready'.

This can continue on – low, low, high, high – but stop before you become dizzy!

Crossing Steps

These consist of one attack together with its parry, every step.

A: 1. Step out R. thrusting low.
B: 1. Cross L. inside as dagger parry of 2, Low L.
B: 2. Step out R. thrusting low.
A: 2. Cross L. inside as dagger parry of 2, Low L.
A: 3. Step out R. thrusting high.
B: 3. Cross behind as dagger parry of 3, High L.
B: 4. Step out R. thrusting high.
A: 4. Cross behind as dagger parry of 3, High L.

Helpful hints: start slowly, building a good rhythm between you. As you get more comfortable and inevitably faster, add a little more distance between each other. Enjoy it, but do keep safe.

Other Dagger Parries

The 'X' Parry

This is the strongest of parries used against cuts, and involves crossing your sword with your dagger; capturing the attacking blade in the leading 'V'.

METHODS
Standing with both weapons held in front of you, raise the points straight up in the air in 'central position 1'; you can now make this 'X' in two ways:

Fig 236

1. To parry to your R., take the dagger over in front of your sword and, pressing the two cross-guards together, angle the joined weapons out R. to present a 'V' to the incoming attack. To parry to your L., from the centre position, take the sword over in front of the dagger and continue as above.
2. Cross the blades in front of your chest, in 'central position 2', and tilt either the sword or the dagger over to the side and 'punch' out.

If there are a series of cutting attacks, return through 'central position 2' before 'punching' out into the next parry.

FOR AN OVERHEAD PARRY
Cross the two weapons in front of you, in 'central position 2', sword behind the dagger, and 'punch' up into the Front High 45 degrees (*see* Fig 236).
  Note: placing the sword behind the dagger enables you to maintain the parry with your dagger, as you can sweep your sword out and around behind your head into your own attack.

FOR A CROTCH PARRY
From 'central position 2', angle the 'X' into the Front Low 45 degrees, and 'punch' down into position.

The Parallel Parry
This is created simply by placing the dagger alongside or parallel (a hand's-breadth away) to the sword when making a parry.

The Replacement Parry
Having parried an attack with your sword, take your dagger over, and replace it in the parry. This frees your sword to attack.

Parry-Beat
Parry the attack with your dagger and, instead of replacing it with the sword, beat your partner's blade off and away from your own dagger.
  To make the beat in the high line, prepare by lifting the point of your sword; in the low line, lower it, and then pass the sword through the 'parallel' position, knocking or beating the attacking blade aside. The whole movement should be free and flowing.
  You can dagger-beat a sword parry too.

Corps-à-Corps Positions

Single Rapier

Fig 237

In his play *Cyrano de Bergerac*, first performed in Paris on 28 December 1897, Edmond de Rostand has Cyrano describe this moment beautifully in the *Ballade* he composes while duelling with de Valvert: '*Les coquilles tintent, ding-don!*' William Hobbs, in the 1990 French film of the same name, creates this moment in his own original way – having Cyrano (Depardieu) throw de Valvert against an iron gate, with the sound of his sword striking it becoming the *ding-don*.

Arriving in a parry, the partners slide the swords down their blades, ending cup-to-cup with a 'Ding!' To steady the grip, they grasp each other's wrists (*see* Fig 237). This typical corps-à-corps position is adopted in the Hollywood swashbuckling movies, to allow for close-ups on the stars for their reactions and dialogue.

Fig 239

Fig 238

Rapier and Dagger
From parries with their daggers, the partners step in, sliding their weapons together hilt-to-hilt (*see* Fig 238).

This can be resolved simply by pushing off away from each other. Alternatively, the partners could circle around a bit, with dialogue, before pushing off.

From the above lock, the right-hand combatant lifts her dagger and her partner's sword up and over (creating a 'bind'), and then locks them together. He supports the lock with his dagger, as if struggling against it (*see* Fig 239).

One way of escaping is to carry out a shoulder or hip barge.

139

Safety note: on coming away from each other, keep your points out front.

Rapier and Cloak

In attack, the cloak can be held at one end and flicked; it can be used to wrap and trap an opponent's leg or arm and blade; or it can even be thrown at the opponent's eyes or over their head.

In defence, it can be wrapped out around your arm, with part left hanging, and so parry sword cuts and thrusts.

Cloak and Two Rapiers
In Fig 240, one partner has caught the end of the other's cloak and is lunging back

Fig 240

Fig 241

in over it. Her partner is cross-stepping to avoid her lunge, and is beginning to circle his sword around his head for a backhand cut.

Cloak and Rapier Against Two Rapiers
In Fig 241, one partner has used the hanging portion of the cloak to parry the other's L.-hand backhand cut, and then used his forearm, protected by the wrapped portion, to parry her R.-hand cut to his head. He replies with a thrust or a cut to her L. knee (the nearest available target).

Generic Rehearsal Sword

If the above rapiers are not available, many drama schools make up a useful rehearsal sword (*see* the blue-handled sword in Fig 242) from sport fencing parts:

* from the epée, a non-electric blade and pommel;
* from the sabre, the handle;
* from the foil, the cup or guard.

Putting it together:

1. The epée blade is triangular with a groove at its base; hold it with the tip facing away from you. Right-handers, turn the blade so that the groove faces left and the top of the triangle faces right (left-handers, reverse this).
2. Put on the cup, with the curved edge facing forwards.
3. Slide the handle on, flat side up.
4. Screw on the pommel and tighten until the blade 'tings'.

Hold the sword by placing your thumb on the flat part of the handle, your forefinger directly under it, both up against the cup-guard. Curl your other fingers lightly back around the handle.

As with a smallsword, when you turn your hand fingernails up, the groove of the blade will be uppermost; when you turn your hand knuckles up, the triangle will be on top. The thumb is opposite the 'true' cutting edge.

References

The rapier and dagger feature prominently in Elizabethan plays such as *Romeo and Juliet* and *Hamlet*. The single rapier is seen in Jacobean plays such as *Cyrano de Bergerac* and *The Three Musketeers*.

Swashbuckling films using the rapier and dagger are few and far between. Errol Flynn adds a dagger to his usual swashbuckling rapier in the film *Don Juan* (much to his

dislike, it is reported). Jean Peters uses a dagger with her sword to effect a neat disarm in *Blackbeard the Pirate*, where Blackbeard is heavily doubled in the fight by the sword-master Fred Cavens.

The single rapier appears in *Le Bossu*, *La Fille de D'Artagnan* and *The Princess Bride*.

SMALLSWORD

The smallsword was so named because it was considerably smaller than the broad-bladed or 'great' swords. Charles II wore a smallsword on his return to England from exile in France, and it remained the civilian sword of fashion into the early 1800s.

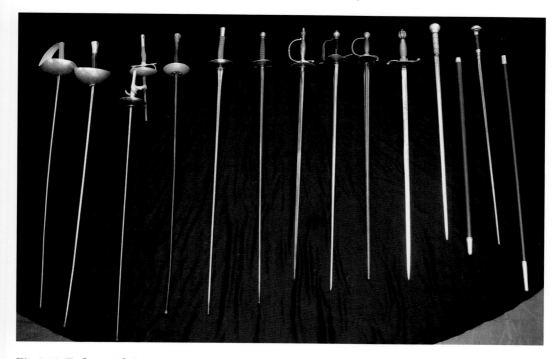

Fig 242 (Left to right): sports swords – sabre; epée; two and a bit foils/grey 'orthopaedic' grip/red Italian style/brown French style; a blue-handled all-purpose training sword. Smallswords: steel replica of a 1700s training smallsword; an antique from the 1800s; a J.P Fournier, Canada; American Armouries; Alan Meek with presentation blade. Swordstick: flat steel; an epée-bladed swordstick.

The smallsword is the lightest of all the swords, and characteristic of the gentry of the period – very elegant and stylish. A gentleman might have had several swords of different designs for different purposes, including a walking-out sword for the day, a sword for going to his club, or dances and balls, a sword to wear at court when attending upon royalty, a sword for funerals and a version, of course, for duelling. This did not necessarily mean that he could or would use it, as Andrew Mahon intimates in his *Art of Fencing* (1735): 'A man who wears a sword without knowing how to use it, is full as ridiculous as a Man who carries Books about with him without knowing how to read.'

Use of the smallsword developed into an elegant sword style, which included side-steps, hand parries and disarms, but before long the weapon was more frequently seen in exercise than for self-defence. While it was deadly in the hands of an expert duellist, it was quickly surpassed in favour of the pistol,

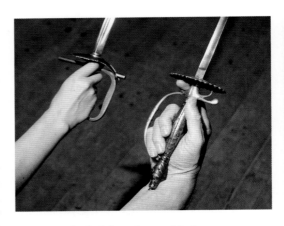

Fig 244 The left-hand sword is in pronation/knuckles up, the guard of - 3; the right-hand sword is in supination/ fingernails up, the guard of - 6.

which anyone, without or without training, could pick up and fire. More often than not, he would fail to hit his target, but at least honour would be satisfied.

As techniques relating to the smallsword reached the height of perfection, its demise as an everyday article of fashionable apparel was just around the corner. By 1774 Sheridan in his play *The Rivals*, set in the fashionable city of Bath, was making the point that 'a sword seen in the streets would create as much alarm as a mad dog'.

Wearing the Smallsword

Suspended from a belt and frog, or over the shoulder by a baldrick, the smallsword was carried at an angle, usually through the back folds of the coat.

Grip

This style of swordplay requires the light, but steely use of the hand, wrist and fingers, with great delicacy and finesse (*see* Fig 244). The hand may be in pronation (knuckles up) or supination (fingernails up).

Fig 243 Wearing the smallsword.

Fig 245

Restoration minuets. The third method of coming on guard relates to ballet.

Step 1: stand in a ballet third position, L. foot pointing out to the Front L. 45 degrees, the R. foot, in front of it, heel back against the instep of the L. foot, pointing out to the Front R. 45 degrees.

Step 2: extend the right foot into the R. diagonal, and pivot the heel out a touch, so that the foot stands facing forwards (12 o'clock).

Step 3: pivot the toes of the L. foot out so that the L. foot faces Side L. 90 degrees.

Step 4: bend the knees and you are on guard (adjust as necessary).

The back hand can still be used to parry attacks such as thrusts, and the sword can therefore be held near or in front of the face as protection (*see* Fig 247, right). It can also, although increasingly less often, be used to hold a cloak, a dagger, even a lantern. Its primary use, however, is as a counter-balance and so is it held up behind the head. This

Salute and On Guard

The opponent is honoured before and after 'play', with the blade to the heart or the lips (*see* Fig 245). As salutes grew in fashion, particularly in the French Court, their use developed into quite an art.

The classical on-guard pose is demonstrated by the Georgian fencer in Fig 246.

In the past, many swordmasters also taught dance, from the days of medieval Morris, through Renaissance court etiquette, to the

Fig 246 The Georgian fencer.

143

Fig 247

The parries come from the two sport fencing weapons: the foil, a thrusting weapon, and the sabre, a cutting weapon, both of which have parries of 5 and 6 (although the 5s guard different parts of the body, as do the 6s). To simplify matters, the foil parry of quinte or 5 was lost (a pronated 4 rarely used nowadays); and the sabre parry of 6 (foil has one already) was changed to 5A, the 'alternative' head parry.

position not only opens the chest, giving style to the pose, but also allows any expensive lace at the wrist to cascade elegantly.

Smallsword fighting is the great-grandfather of sport fencing and many of the techniques have not altered much since the 1700s. In fact, it still provides most of the basics of sport foil fencing. Many of the original French terms are retained, too.

The weapon is shorter and lighter than the rapier, and so the movements are both smaller and faster. Parries are designed to deflect an in-coming attack, enabling immediate riposte. Indeed, in some cases, the defender relies on the attacker's forward momentum to carry them on to their extended weapon.

Parries

The various international societies and academies that teach stage fighting today, tend to use a common numbering system for the eight main parries:

Fig 248 Parries 1 - 2 - 3.

Fig 249 Parries 4 - 5 - 5A.

* Low-line parries of: 1 and 2 – 7 and 8.
* High-line parries of: 3 and 4 – 6.
* Overhead parries of: 5 and 5A.

Parry 1 – Prime or 'Watch Parry': protects the L. side of your body, Low to High (inside). It is the first parry on drawing your sword. Thumb down, 'looking at the watch on your wrist', knuckles facing you.

Parry 2 – Seconde or 'Actor's Parry': protects Low R. (outside). Thumb on the inside, knuckles up.

Parry 3 – Tierce: protects High R. (outside). Thumb on the inside, knuckles up.

Parry 4 – Quarte: protects High L. (inside). Thumb on the inside, fingernails up.

Parry 5 – Quinte: protects the head, blade horizontal or sloping. Thumb underneath, knuckles facing you. (For the crotch parry, lower the head parry of 5 down to the Fwd. Low 45 degrees.)

Parry 5A – 'Window Parry': the alternative head parry. Thumb underneath, fingernails facing you.

Parry 6 – Sixte: protects High R. (outside). Thumb to the R., fingernails up.

Parry 7 – Septime: protects Low L. (inside). Thumb to the R., fingernails up.

Parry 8 – Octave: protects the Low R. (outside). Thumb to the R., fingernails up.

Basic parries are achieved by taking your hand straight across, or in a half-circle down or up, to meet the oncoming attack – to deflect its energy into another line. Circular parries become very much more effective with a lighter and more manoeuvrable sword. These parries pick up the attack in one line, and,

145

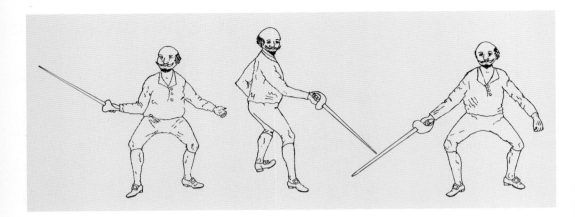

Fig 250 Parries 6 - 7 - 8.

instead of deflecting it into another, they circle round inside the attack and then move it outside the body, allowing the attacker's energy to continue on in the same line.

All these parries can be adapted to the weapon and period of choice.

Evasions Designed to Counter-Attack

Fig 251 shows a full volte. Spinning halfway around, the combatant has thrust her back leg, her left, towards the opponent, as she thrusts with the sword. (My teacher, Henry Marshall, aptly called this move 'bum in face'.)

Fig 251

Fig 252

This is one of the few occasions where the hand position is with the thumb down, the palm out to the side.

In Fig 252, the fighter has evaded a high thrusting attack by reverse-lunging, taking his right foot deeply back. This Italian move is known as the Passata Sotto, and is a favourite against a 'pushy' opponent. Fred Cavens uses a sideways version of this as a 'kill' move for Errol Flynn in his swashbuckling movies, *Captain Blood* and *Don Juan*.

Disarms

Methods of disarming were still being taught even when most gentlemen of the day pre-ferred the 'play with blunts' as opposed to 'fresh air and sharps'.

Figs 253 and 254 show two historic tech-niques, which involve the volte, to close in to the opponent. If the opponent does not give in or give up their sword, they will be in big trouble!

Fig 253 Disarm after Angelo.

Fig 254

The right-hand fighter voltes in, taking the blade of his own sword in his L. hand; seizes his opponent's sword hand, with his R. trapping her, and finishes threatening to stab her. This one looks great!

Moves such as these may be seen in the film and play of *Les Liaisons Dangereuses*, and the films *Le Bossu* and *The Duellists*.

OTHER SWORDS

The Military Sabre

The blades of the sabre are curved or straight, light or heavy, depending on the regiment. Real military swords are more likely to be used as decoration, as part of a uniform. Today, many of the blades used for theatrical fighting are made from aluminium (*see* Fig 255).

The Naval Cutlass

Because it was for use on board ship, this sword had a blade that was shorter (45 to 67cm/18 to 27in) than that of its military cousin, and was straight or curved. In 1889 a 70-cm (28-in) blade was adopted – intended to become standard – with a large curved knuckle-guard.

The theatrical cutlass originally had a cavalry sword blade cut to size, but today many of the blades are made from aluminium. A naval cutlass might be called for in films or plays such as *Peter Pan*, *The Pirates of Penzance*, *Treasure Island* or a pantomime version of *Robinson Crusoe*. For further research, you might want to refer to the booklet *Naval Cutlass Exercise*, by John McGrath and Mark Barton of the Royal Navy Amateur Fencing Association. Its objective, in the words of the association's president, Admiral Sir Alan West, KCB, DSC, 'is to trace and record the strands that go to make up the story of formalised provision for training in swordsmanship from the first recorded mention in 1733'.

In the 'disarm after Angelo', the right-hand combatant, having parried the other's sword, grasps his wrist, makes a three-quarter volte, and ends threatening me with her point.

Fig 254 shows a potential disarm, the 'Seizure of both Sword and Person – after De Liancour', as shown in Alfred Hutton's *Old Sword Play*. De Liancour has created this move as a method of dealing with an adversary who rushes in with the intention of stabbing.

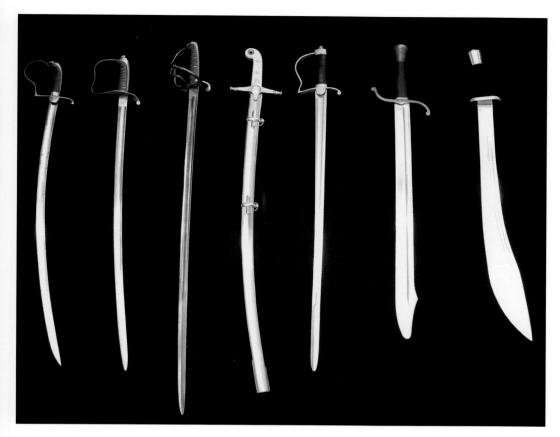

Fig 255 Left to right: five military sabres; a falchion; a Chinese broadsword.

The Hanger

The hanger is a sword with a short, curved blade suited for cutting and slashing – patterned in European hunting swords – a personal civilian sidearm, named for the style in which it was worn, 'hanging' straight down by the side.

HOLLYWOOD STYLE

Fred Cavens, a graduate of the Belgian Military Institute of Physical Education and Fencing, was the primary swordmaster in Hollywood from the late 1920s through to the 1950s, working with such stars as Douglas Fairbanks Snr and Jnr, Errol Flynn, Basil Rathbone, Cornel Wilde, Tyrone Power, Jean Peters and Maureen O'Hara.

In an interview, he said, 'All movements, instead of being as small as possible, as in competitive fencing, must be large but nevertheless correct. Magnified is the word. The routine should contain the most spectacular attacks and parries it is possible

149

Fig 256 Left to right: latex hand axe; Star Wars Mace Windu *light-sabre; one of Sorcha's swords from* Willow; *latex sword; latex two-headed axe; two latex swords; foam sword, dagger and shield from Toys R Us.*

to execute while remaining logical to the situation. In other words, the duel should be a fight and not a fencing exhibition.'

His cutting attacks seem to be based on military sabre techniques, while much of the point-work derives from the epée and the foil.

The following sequences are inspired by observation of some of Cavens' swashbuckling films, including *Don Juan, Robin Hood, The Sons of the Musketeers, Anne of the Indies, Against all Flags.*

Helpful hints: blade contact is to be made in

the middle, between the two fighters, the attacks 'bouncing back' off each other.

1. High Twos: a series of cutting attacks by both fighters in the high line, using alternate forehand and backhand cuts, your hand in front of you, the sword tip circling around your head.
2. Side Twos: a series of cutting attacks on the side, which go from a high backhand (to the cheek) to a low backhand (to the knee).

3. Wheel twos: the attacker brings his sword back, making an inside circle, into a backhand cut across between the two partners, to his right. The defender performs an inside rising parry of 1, circling forwards into the same backhand cut across between the partners, to his right. The attacker then makes an inside rising parry of 1, circling forwards into a backhand cut across between them, and so on.

4. Square fours: from his right, the attacker makes a forehand wheel cut down across between the partners, to his opponent's right. The defender performs a rising parry of 8/sloping 5A into a forehand cut on the same side (to the opponent's left). The attacker performs a rising parry of 1 into a backhand cut across to the defender's left. The defender makes a rising parry of 1 into a backhand cut on the same side (to the opponent's right). The attacker then performs a rising parry of 8/sloping 5A into a forehand cut, and so on.

VICTORIAN STANDARD COMBATS

Following some years of research, my teacher

Fig 257

Henry Marshall established the theory that Victorian standard combats evolved among actors without the aid of a fencing master, being based on real sword moves, wrongly remembered. There were no real attacks or parries and so the routines were easy to perform, with both actors making the same moves together. In fact, it was only possible to identify the attacker by seeing who was advancing.

Each routine was named after the number of strokes in it: the Threes, the Fives, the Skeleton Sevens, the Round Eights, the Glasgow Tens, the Long Elevens.

The Threes form the core of the odd-numbered routines. The following routine is influenced by Cavens, who invariably finishes a phrase with a backhand cut in the high line:

Both partners adopt the on-guard position with their blades held across them, knuckles up.

Cut 1: both swing the point around their head into a forehand cut high.

Cut 2: both swing back around their head, and drop to a backhand cut low.

Cut 3: both pull the sword back, then forward to a backhand cut high.

The partners return to their starting positions on guard.

The other odd-numbered routines are arrived at by simply adding in High Twos or Side Twos.

The best weapon for this is a sport fencing sabre. The children's No. 2 blade is particulary suitable because it is slightly shorter than the adult one, and therefore more manageable in large groups.

KNIVES

The knife is a weapon, generally with a blade of less than 45cm (18in), that is as varied, in style, as the sword. There is a long list of types:

the bowie knife; the stiletto; the cinqueda; the flick knife; any kind of kitchen knife; the medieval or Renaissance dagger; the navaja; the dirk; the sheath knife; the kukri; the commando knife; the butterfly knife; and even a bayonet (*see* Fig 259).

In reality, knife-fighting is a scary business, not the least because it is up close and personal. Distance gives you time and the opposite holds equally true. Close-up, everything happens really fast.

As with every other fight in the theatre that is physical story-telling, knife-fighting involves big preparations, large body movements and choreographed moves. It is however, as different from a 'real' knife-fight, as it is to a knife-fight in the films.

Fig 258

The first step of the preparation is to blunt the knife, whether it is wood, aluminium or metal, so that there is no danger of scratching, cutting or causing damage of any kind if there should be any contact. To double the safety, clear tape can be placed over the blunted edge. (*See* pages 181–184, on preparation and maintenance.)

Rubber, aluminium and wooden training knives are available on the internet and plastic ones can be found in toy shops.

Holding the Knife

There are four positions to consider for now:

1. as if holding the bottom end of a stick, blade pointing up, cutting edge facing forwards (*see* Fig 257, left);
2. as if holding the top of a stick with the blade pointing down, cutting edge facing back to you (*see* Fig 258, left); the other partner has the same grip but has reversed her arm as in a medieval pose from Talhoffer;
3. with the blade pointing back along the outside of your forearm, the cutting edge facing outwards (*see* Fig 257, right), often seen as a 'Special Forces' grip;
4. the blade pointing forwards, as if pointing a torch at someone, thumb on top as in the 'sabre grip' (*see* page 113). This grip allows the most variety of movement and is probably the one most associated with a knife-fighter.

The first and second grips are basic 'natural' stabbing positions, for stabbing up and for stabbing down. They can reasonably be categorized as 'untrained' moves or perhaps 'frenzied' (as in the film *Psycho*).

On Guard

With the knife in your R. hand, with the blade pointing forwards, stand in R. on guard, knees bent, your arms in front of you. The free hand acts as a counter-balance and a possible distraction.

Horizontal Slashes

When making horizontal slashes, think of a cobra, and weave the knife from side to side. Lead with the cutting edge by turning your wrist. Next, add the body, leading from the legs and rib-cage. As you cut or slash through, your free hand should move as well, in opposition.

To avoid an attack using horizontal slashes, the victim must remove the target, and react depending on which part of the body is under attack:

* to the stomach – jump back, remembering to lift the arms and hands back as well; if you leave them in front of you, they may be cut instead;
* to the head – duck straight down under the slash, or, as in the film *The Matrix*, lean back following the pathway of the knife;
* to the lower legs – lift the leg out of the way, or jump over the knife; it may be a bit of a cliché, but why not if you are young and vigorous.

Diagonal Slashes

When making diagonal slashes, high to low and low to high, use your whole body. (Refer back to the sword cutting diagram on page 120.)

To avoid such an attack, angle your body, lean away to the side – you can face in, or away, with the top half of your body, but try and keep your eyes focused on the whole attack. It is dangerous to watch the blade of the knife only, as you may become mesmerized by it and unable to react.

Blocks and Counter-Moves

You can parry an attack with your own knife,

but it is more usual to block using your free hand or forearm against the attacker's knife-hand, wrist or forearm. Stop the attack or cause it to pass you by.

Counter-moves can include slashing back at the attacker, so that they have to move away to avoid; grasp the opponent's knife wrist and throw it down and away between you; while holding the attacker's wrist, try to slice their forearm with your knife.

For an unarmed defence against a stab down on to the head, first make an 'X' block, with your R. forearm over the L. (if attacked by a right-hander). 'Punch' it up into the High Fwd. 45 degrees, and then proceed into a counter-move:

1. step in alongside the attacker and, using your R. hand, throw him using the Irish whip (see page 101);
2. step around behind him, taking his arm into a back hammer arm-lock (see page 72), and disarm him; or
3. slip your L. arm around inside his elbow and, with your R. forearm, 'push' forwards, against his wrist, past his shoulder. This arm-lock will take him to the floor. Walk alongside him and support him, as he sits, chin on chest, and rolls back to lie down. Once he is down, you can remove his knife.

Wound or Kill

The victim is finished off by a forward stab that is very like a punch.

Set up the illusion by letting the audience 'see' the point approaching the victim's body. At the last second, when it is out of their view, turn the hand sideways as if punching – knuckles up or down – and lightly make contact, if necessary.

Safety note: do not turn the knife so that the point is up, as this is potentially very dangerous.

The victim reacts as if he has been punched, being careful to keep his head up away from the knife.

The attacker continues the move by pulling his arm back away, making sure that, when at a safe distance, he straightens his knife hand again, so that it appears that the point of the blade is coming out of the victim.

Throat-Cuts

The victim having his throat cut must be on balance throughout and it is an excellent idea for the attacker to stand close behind him, giving body support.

The preparation is similar to that for the neck break (see page 64). The attacker tilts the head of the victim straight back with his L. hand, exposing the throat. For greater effect, he can turn the head to the side (with the victim in control), in the opposite direction to the knife.

Safety note: be careful of the men's Adam's Apple, cutting above or below it.

Holding the knife, the attacker uses his thumb to make light contact against the exposed throat and draws his hand around. If the victim's head is to one side, it is then turned into the slice. There is no need to make real contact with the knife for a straight throat-cut illusion, unless laying blood on the neck (see below). Indeed, it is better not to make contact with the knife if you have been fighting with it before the throat-cut, for its edges may have become splintered.

Blood Knives

Blood knives come with fixed or retractable blades.

The version with the firm blade has a tube inside it, running from the handle to a hole either at the point or halfway down the blade. The blood is contained either in the handle or in a bulb on the end (pommel). Squeezing it forces the blood down and out of the tube. The knife may also have an absorbent material between the edges of the blade, which is soaked in fake blood or perhaps red make-up or lipstick. When the throat is 'cut', this leaves a red line on the skin.

The retractable blade is pushed in, down the hollow handle, on contact. On the inside end of the blade is a plunger that forces the blood, stored in the handle, back through a tube and out, via holes in the small cross-guard, to squirt on to the target.

Safety note: mis-handling, dropping, or even stabbing inaccurately, can cause the blade to bend and consequently, it will not re-tract when it should. 'Ouch !'

Protective padding should be worn under the victim's costume if at all possible. The 'stab' does require a certain amount of pressure to squeeze the 'blood' out of the knife and you cannot simply rely on well-toned stomach muscles.

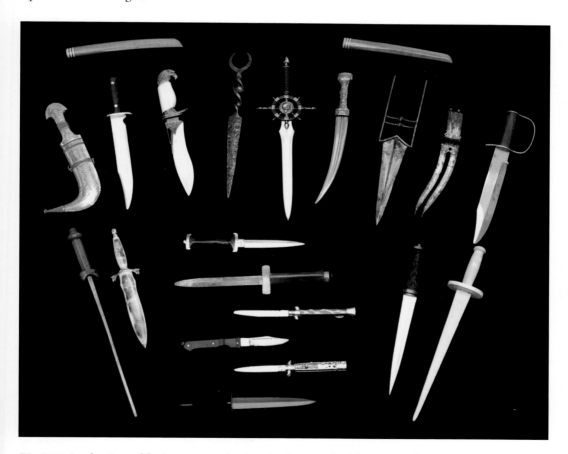

Fig 259 A selection of knives, some single-edged, some double; some ethnic, some fantasy; some theatrical. They vary in composition from steel to wood, plastic to foam. There is a retractable dagger (brown handle) in the centre set of horizontal knives. The tube is just visible under the leather binding (a lighter strip) on the top of the handle.

155

STICKS

Popular during the Middle Ages, the quarter-staff (the name has no definite origin) was carried, in the main, by the 'common man' (such as those who feature prominently in the film *Robin Hood, Prince of Thieves*). It was of a length of between 1.8 and 2.75m (6 and 9ft), often bound with iron bands at either end.

The techniques of the halberd, spear and, much later, the rifle and bayonet have been adapted from its use, although by the end of the nineteenth century the quarterstaff, as a military weapon, had long become obsolete. However, according to Terry Brown, in his book *English Martial Arts*, its use was 'still valued as a manly sport with good character-building qualities'. Indeed, at the turn of the twentieth century, Baden-Powell and his Boy Scouts were still practising quarterstaff drills with a five-foot ash staff.

In theatre and for teaching, I favour a 1.8m (6-ft) staff of bamboo or rattan rather than ash, oak or other hardwoods.

Before you use any new weapon, get to know it. How heavy or light is it? Where is its point of balance? Does it have a rough or smooth surface? Will it splinter or break easily on contact or if dropped? One of the best ways of getting used to the feel of the staff is to twirl it around, from its centre, or from its end. (*Note:* twirling from the end, you are going to need a very big space indeed, if you are to avoid hitting anyone.) A wide range of staff-twirling exercises can be used, adapted from many disciplines, including Beijing Opera spear-fighting and flag- or baton-twirling.

There are two main fighting forms: short form and long form.

Short Form

Holding the Staff
With the staff sideways on, place both hands so that the staff is divided into three equal lengths. The grip can be over or under, with the hands held the same or in opposition. Exercise your grip on the staff by changing the hand positions and, rather than let go completely, keep one hand still, maintaining a light contact, and 'slip' your other hand around as you change grip or slide it further up or down the staff.

Routines
Do the following moves together at the same time (Hollywood style).

Helpful hints: hold the staff relatively loosely. If you grip the staff tightly, the end will curve dangerously in towards your partner.

SEQUENCE 1: THE SQUARE
This sequence begins with your R. hands creating the 'right-hand square', but it can just as easily start with the L.

Feet are about hip-width apart. The partners stand about three paces apart, holding the staff in front of them comfortably at chest height.

To make the attacks:

Step 1: extend your R. hands towards the outside of your partner's head, High R. The top third, or fore-end, of your staffs cross in the middle between you, at roughly head height.

Fig 260

Fig 261

Step 2: pull back from the strike, at the same time extending the lower third, or butt-end, forwards, to meet in the same place, High L. (*see* Fig 260).

For the second half of the drill, lower the staff to hip height.

Step 3: extend the fore-end forwards to the outside of your partner's knees, Low R. (*see* Fig 261).

Step 4: pull it back from the strike as you extend the butt-end to meet in the same place, Low L.

Helpful hints: the moves should be aimed, as if punching, straight towards the outside of the target, rather than being circular, as in 'canoeing'.

At this early stage the moves should be done smoothly, in rhythm, without force (you can only build speed with a light touch).

The feet are added, in opposition, one step per strike, going forwards and backwards. The partners can then try circling round each other.

SEQUENCE 2: THE VERTICAL 'X' OR '+'
Footwork: while the following four moves can be done standing still, it is more comfortable

and more efficient if each strike is accompanied by a passing step (as when using the broadsword).

Attacker: step forwards, R. foot for a R. strike and L. for L.

Defender: step backwards, L. foot back to make a L. parry and R. foot back to make a R. parry.

Two side-strikes are made to the flank (the side of the rib-cage area). The attacker starts, as above, with the staff held across the centre of his body. With the R. hand, he extends the fore-end, horizontally towards his partner's L. flank. As he pulls the R. back, extending the butt-end with his L. to his partner's R. flank.

The defender parries to her L. side by lowering the L. (butt-end) of her staff, lifting the R. (fore-end) up, and turning her whole body, pushing the staff in its vertical position, out into the Front L. 45 degrees (*see* Fig 262, right).

Helpful hints: the quickest way to parry to your R. side, is not to move the staff but to swivel the top half of your body straight across to face Front R. 45 degrees, taking your R. foot back.

If you have more time, swivel the staff in a half-circle to the R. by dropping the R. hand and raising the L. into the vertical, before turning to face the other side. (This looks good too.)

Fig 262

Fig 263

Safety note: as these parries are with the centre of the staff, you need to open your grip on the staff a little wider to prevent being struck on the knuckles.

Next, the attacker makes two vertical strikes – one to the head and one to the crotch (straight up the middle).

From the side attack, above, the attacker half-circles the butt-end (L. end) up and forwards to the centre of his partner's head, straightening his L. arm. Simultaneously, he pulls the fore-end back into his R. hip area (*see* Fig 263, left). As he half-circles the staff, he passes forwards on to his L. foot to arrive just before the strike.

The defender parries by lifting the staff up in the High Fwd. 45 degrees.

To attack the crotch from the above head attack, the attacker lifts the staff up off his partner's, and passes his R. leg forwards. This will drive his R. hand and the fore-end of the staff towards the opponent's crotch.

Note: it is very important to extend your punch straight down to the target and not to curve the strike up, which will happen if you have bent arms.

The defender parries straight down from overhead, opening the legs sideways rather than leaving the front knee centre and vulnerable.

THE BIND
The bind is a connecting move that allows the partners to create a short routine using the two sequences described above. The flight path of a bind is a half-circle.

From the last move in a R.-hand square, you will have your L. hands forwards in the low line; one of the partners will now lead the bind. Both partners fix their back (R.) hands in the area of their R. hips, and then the 'leader' of the bind will, with a straight L. arm, sweep the butt-end of his staff to the R., up, over and around, to end at waist height on the L. side.

Helpful hints: the leader should concentrate on creating as large a 'rainbow' as possible. The follower concentrates on keeping the end of his staff connected to a single spot on the leader's staff, maintaining a slight pressure in opposition, to keep the fore-end from sliding up and off, or down on to the leader's knuckles.

The Entire Routine
First sequence: R.-hand square 1 – 2 – 3 – 4, ending Low L. with both butt-ends forwards.
Connecting move: attacker binds the staffs up and over, to Side L.
Second sequence: side attacks 5 – 6, passing the feet forwards R. L.; and into the R. Head attack on the R. foot – 7, followed by the L. crotch attack, on the L. foot – 8.
Defender: use the appropriate parries, passing back during the second sequence.

A Finishing Move
A strike to the toe is a good finishing move. Pull the staff back up off the parry a little way and, using the top hand, drive the point down, 'bouncing' it back off the floor, just beside the toe of your partner. Your partner reacts by jumping back, lifting the 'struck' toe. 'Ow!'

All the above strikes can, of course, be combined in different sequences to create your own routines.

Long Form

Holding the Staff
Your dominant hand will be holding the butt-end of the staff to your side at hip level, while your other hand, in an under-grip about one-third of the way down, will be comfortably held in front of you (*see* Fig 262, left).

Using the Staff
If the staff is of a bendy material, it is quite possible to use the tip to 'beat' in any direction, either in attack or in defence.

Thrusting can be done in two ways:

1. bayonet-style thrusting: holding your front arm extended in front of you, using both hands, 'jab' the point forwards; you can parry in the same way, by using the top-third of the staff to knock your partner's thrusting attack to either side;
2. Chinese-style spear thrusting: use your extended front arm, palm up in an under-grip, as a 'fixed point' (similar to using a cue playing snooker or pool), through which your back hand pushes the staff forwards. A full thrust will end with the back hand hard up against the hand of the extended front arm. You can make simple parries with a slight sideways movement of the front hand and you can even make circular parries.

Staffs feature in the *Robin Hood* films; the classic scene is the fight between Robin Hood and Little John with quarterstaffs on a log over a stream. In *Against All Flags*, Errol Flynn fights on a pirate ship with 'boarding pikes' or boathooks, while in *Rumble in the Bronx*, Jackie Chan uses a ski to great effect. In *Star Wars:*

The Phantom Menace, the scene to watch is the Sith's fight against the two Jedi Masters.

CANES

While a stick is straight, a cane has a curved handle. French cane fighting was all the rage in the late 1800s, the sword having seemingly disappeared from the streets. In fact, many of the 'canes' carried by members of the upper classes were sword-sticks. Today, such sticks are considered to be 'concealed weapons' and it is therefore illegal to carry them on the streets.

For reference, *see* E.W. Barton-Wright's 1899 *The Bartitsu Compendium* (edited by Tony Wolf), which 'combined the four most effective close-combat styles known at the time: ko-ryu Jiujitsu, French Savate, scientific boxing and self-defence with a walking stick'. In addition, a number of martial arts movies use the cane as a training weapon.

WEAPONS OF OPPORTUNITY

Weapons of opportunity can be anything that may be 'discovered' during the scene (kitchen utensils) or on the set (furniture, chairs, the door of a fridge), or other props, such as telephones. Their use can make for a very exciting and seemingly naturalistic fight. However, first you need to ask yourself several questions. Is it safe, possible, practical and repeatable – in other words, will it last the rigours of rehearsal and performance ? (Most kitchen utensils will work but a packet of Cornflakes may have to be replaced for every show.)

Having used the 'weapon', what are the repercussions? Broken bits of vase, plate or glass, spilt liquids or scattered Cornflakes may constitute a danger to the actors as the scene continues. What can be done about it?

Safety note: it is necessary when working with 'discovered' objects to be extra-vigilant with regard to the safety aspects. Familiarize yourself with the item:

* Look for obvious dangers, including rough, jagged or pointed edges. Is it breakable, creating nasty splinters?
* How does it feel when you pick it up? Is it smooth or rough, floppy or solid, heavy or fragile?
* In what ways can you practically hold it ? Do you need one or two hands and how good is your grip on it?
* How does it move? Where is its point of balance? How much space does it need?
* If it has a flexible element, for example, a telephone cord, how do all the relative bits move and react when fighting and how many ways of there of using it?
* If you want to throw it, is it safe, possible, practical? A cushion may be OK, but what about a vase of flowers?

It is both fun and challenging to discover an object's potential use but it will take more rehearsal time. You may discover new ways of working, but, equally, you may discover that you have to return to the basic techniques of attack and defence (which tend to be universal).

There are a number of questions to ask in the first instance:

* What kind of attack would suit the object? Is it a crunch, poke or slice weapon, or is it best used for indirect actions such as distracting or disabling, binding or blinding, tripping or entrapping? Which parts of the victim's body are particularly vulnerable to the weapon?
* What kind of defence will be applicable?
* What reactions – both physical and vocal – will follow?

You will need to have exact duplicate spares available for the rehearsals, particularly with the smaller objects, and, if they work, for the performances.

In working with such objects, you will need to explore slowly, using all the stage combat fundamentals. You need to be ready to accept that, in the end, such a weapon may not be practical. It may cause more problems than the effect is worth, or it may not be safely repeatable.

If you find that it does work, then, as with all stage combat, you can build the tempo of the fight gradually throughout the rehearsal period until you reach 'performance' speed. Continue to keep an eye on the object, and get the stage management to check it carefully for wear and tear before every performance.

For reference, watch the films of Jackie Chan, who is a master at making a weapon or a 'shield' out of objects discovered in his environment, as well as the fight in the kitchen in *Kill Bill Vol. I.*

GUNS

'Nothing beats a firearm for instant destructive power', writes Alan Suddeth in his book *Fight Directing for the Theatre.* The history of the development of gunpowder and of guns also makes for fascinating reading; these 'point-and-pull' tools and their oh-so-final 'poke' seem to have a powerful appeal.

You may come across any of the following weapons:

* matchlocks, used by Civil War (1640s) re-enactment groups;
* flintlocks, used by re-enactors of the Napoleonic War (late 1700s to early 1800s);
* percussion cap pistols and revolvers, used by Western and American Civil War re-enactors (1860s);

Fig 264

* revolvers and semi-automatics, the weapons of the 1900s.
* automatics – primarily military;
* shotguns – in use today by those who have a licence, but a deactivated one (with its own special licence) is best for the theatre.

When you come across a reference in a play to one of the weapons listed above, you need to ask yourself a number of questions. Do you really need a firearm on stage? Can you do without it? If not, does it need to be fired on stage? If not, then you can use a non-firing replica or a deactivated firearm. If you are convinced that a shot needs to be fired, does it have to be on stage? Could it be done in the wings, or could a sound-effect be used?

Remember, in a small space, or in close proximity, gunfire can damage a person's hearing. If necessary, re-think live firing on stage. Perhaps you could use a smaller-calibre weapon, with a 'quieter' blank? In addition to these considerations, many theatre companies

Fig 265 (Left, top to bottom): a fantasy pistol based on the one beneath it, a typical Scottish all-steel flintlock pistol; a locally purpose-built percussion-cap pistol with no barrel; the lowest is a Glock 9mm semi-automatic blank firer. (Right, top to bottom): a Second World War British Army deactivated Webley .38; a 1908 pattern Colt .45 blank firer (made in Italy); the black pistol is a rubber model of a 9mm Walther PPK; and the last is a silver 'Cowboy-style' Colt .45 blank-firing revolver.

will now permit the use only of a wooden, plastic or rubber pistol, which you can buy from martial arts shops, or on the internet.

If a firearm really does need to be fired on stage, and you are at all unsure about the use of firearms, get the advice of someone with practical knowledge of, and training in, their use.

Golden rules of safety: never play with a gun in fun; do not wave it around; do not point it at anyone other than within the dictates of the scene, and then only under careful supervision in rehearsal. At all times be mindful of the dangers.

The Pistol

Holding the Pistol
Keep the pistol at arm's length, out away from your face and body.

Fashion dictates how you hold a pistol. A modern-day approach is shown in Fig 264 (left), with the pistol being held in the right hand, the left hand underneath the butt, supporting it. With knees bent, the actor is on balance and ready to fire. Remember, eyes and gun, look and point in the same direction; aim with your body.

In complete contrast, the actor to the right has adopted a stance appropriate to a nineteenth-century duel – sideways on to reduce the chance of being hit, sighting along the top of the barrel.

Firing Blanks
Everyone's safety lies in believing that all guns are loaded! Everyone involved must also be aware that blanks can blind, burn or disfigure, or kill.

Ear defenders should be supplied for anyone who is around the gun when it is fired in rehearsal. On stage, ear plugs should be given to as many of the actors as possible. This also applies in the wings for the 'designated' person

(*see* below) who is firing the pistol, and for anyone who has to be near that person. The wings can sometimes be more crowded that the stage.

A space should be cleared for firing.

All stage guns will have their barrels blocked so that no projectile or powder can come out forwards.

Flintlocks, Muskets and Pistols

These kind of weapons are used in plays such as *Treasure Island*. To fire for 'real' they have to be loaded with black powder and ball, which are put down the barrel. (To learn more, read any of the *Sharpe* books by Bernard Cornwell, or join a 'Black Powder' re-enactment group – *see* 'Bibliography'.)

The powder would be ignited by a percussion cap and these can be obtained for stage use. They give a sharp crack when struck and work fine as a 'gunshot' on stage.

Revolvers

Revolvers have a revolving chamber into which you put the blanks. When fired, the expanding gas, flame, smoke and gunpowder residue comes out either side of the chamber, sometimes up to a distance of about 1.2m (4ft), depending on the strength of the blank.

Nothing comes out back behind the chamber, so, as long as the person firing the gun keeps it at arm's length pointed away from them, they should be safe.

Semi-Automatics

The blanks are loaded into a magazine housed in the butt or grip of the pistol and, when fired, the gun will use part of the gas to re-set the whole firing mechanism, pushing the next round into the barrel and cocking the hammer, ready for you to pull the trigger.

If you keep on pulling the trigger, the gun will continue its action until all the ammunition is expended, leaving the gun locked open.

Safety note: the empty cartridge cases are forcibly ejected up and out to the right side of the barrel. Be careful where you stand when firing or 'making safe', in relation to other actors and to the audience.

To reload, it is out with the magazine, in with the new, release the lock, and the gun is ready to fire again. In films, this action is often done by actors, but it takes a lot of practice to get it smooth and right. There should be an armourer on set to explain it all to those who need the information.

Looking After Guns

A deactivated gun is a real gun that cannot fire. It should always be accompanied by a special licence stating where, when and by whom it was deactivated.

On first getting hold of a gun, always check to see whether or not it is loaded – it should not be. Very occasionally, hired guns are sent with a full chamber, so it is vital always to check.

There should be one person – the 'designated person' – who is in charge of the weapon at all times, for rehearsal and performance. That person must have all the practical training that the actor has and will also be responsible for the following:

* loading, if done off stage. If the actor has to load the gun on stage, make sure that they know how to do it safely and correctly;
* handing the weapon to the actor before he or she enters the stage; for a revolver, they must swing open the cylinder and show the actor whether it is empty or full; for semi-automatics, they must tell the actor if it is 'ready to go', if the 'Safety' is on, and whether or not they need to 'cock' the gun before firing;
* collecting the weapon when the actor leaves the stage; an actor must never leave a loaded gun on the props table or lying around in the dressing room;

* unloading, maintaining and storing the gun.

First Firing

1. Make sure that anyone close has ear defenders.
2. Give a verbal warning to the room in general that a gun is going off. In a theatre, when gunshots are being fired in rehearsal, a warning can be put out over the tannoy and the Stage Door may be alerted as well, so that they can field any outside queries.
3. Demonstrate the firing to the actor, so they can observe the effect of the gunshot from a safe distance.
4. Then teach the actor how to fire the gun and, give them time to practice so they are comfortable.

If the firing takes place as a result of, say, a struggle, make sure that it is all rehearsed on the set without blanks, shouting 'Bang' at the moment of firing.

Handling the Gun

It may be very easy to pull the trigger (a hair-trigger) or it might take some effort. Make sure you find out when it is unloaded! Keep the trigger finger off – lay it alongside until the time comes to fire it. You may need to cock the gun before it will fire or pull back the slide on a semi-automatic. You should also check whether or not there is a 'Safety' catch, and if it is it 'on' or 'off'.

Use the correct-sized blanks for the gun – get new ones for a show – and never re-use a blank that has failed to go off. Dispose of it safely.

Back-Up Plan

In case the blank fails to ignite, or the gun freezes in mid-action or jams, you must have a back-up plan. On leaving the stage, the actor must remember to hand the firearm over to the designated person, and let them know that it has misfired.

The designated person should be in the wings with a back-up gun ready to fire should the actor's gun fail go off. Alternatively, he could be ready with a recorded sound-effect, or the actors could create their own sound, slap-stick-style.

Making Safe

Revolvers
Press or push the cylinder release catch and swing out or remove the cylinder from the frame and eject the blanks. Remember that, when a blank has been fired, the heated cartridge expands, so it may be a tight fit in the chamber.

Semi-Automatics
Remove the magazine, then, holding the top of the weapon away from your face, smartly pull the slide back three times. Any blank or casing left in the chamber should be ejected. Even so, always visually check to make sure the breech is empty.

Storing the Gun
The gun should be stored in a safe that is bolted to the floor and in the office of a 'responsible' person (for example, the Stage Manager). The ammunition should also be locked away. In an ideal world, the ammunition and the magazine, or chamber of the revolver, should be stored separately from the gun, making it twice as hard for any would-be thief to steal a complete weapon.

If a gun is stolen or mislaid and cannot be found, the police must be informed.

Guns: Points to Remember
* Check the current laws about the use of firearms on stage.
* Hire a gun from a reputable armourer.
* If in any doubt about its use, consult an expert.
* Impress upon everyone the fact that guns are not toys.
* Have a 'designated person' in total charge of the gun.
* Warn the audience that there is to be gun-fire on stage, with signs in the foyer and the programme.
* Keep all weapons and ammunition in a safe when not in use.
* If a gun is stolen or lost, report it to the police.

4 WAITING IN THE WINGS

'I have always wanted my work to have the lightness and joy of a Springtime – which never lets anyone suspect the labour it has cost.'

(Henri Matisse)

CHOREOGRAPHY/ FIGHT ARRANGING/ FIGHT DIRECTING

Beginnings

Whether you call yourself a fight choreographer, arranger or director, a swordmaster or maître-des-armes, battle co-ordinator, chief mischief maker or creator of organized chaos, you still have to start somewhere. Begin by asking yourself a few questions:

* What is the story?
* Who are the characters? What is their part in the story?
* Why do the characters interact in this way?
* What is the result of their conflict?

In terms of fighting style, you need to know whether the characters have had any training at all, and in what particular style? For example, in Shakespeare's *Twelfth Night*, Sir Andrew Ague-Cheek may have had some training with

(Opposite) The Musketeer.

a sword, being a Gentleman, but Viola, a girl masquerading as a boy, is unlikely ever to have held a sword, let alone to know what to do with it. The period of the play is important, too. A policeman making an arrest in an Agatha Christie play might simply lay a restraining arm on the villain's shoulder with a sotto voce remark such as, 'You're nicked, old son!' In contrast, today's police are highly trained in various restraining and disabling techniques and their approach might be slightly more physical.

The Moves of the Fight

Fights have a beginning, a middle and an end.

What sparks off the fight and who makes the first attack? Is it an all-out attempt to finish the fight with that one blow – a knock-out punch, or a swift disabling thrust – or is the intention merely to scare the opponent away? Sometimes, neither protagonist wants to get involved but it is unavoidable. One excellent example of a fight between two male suitors who do not want to fight, do not know how to fight, and certainly never have fought before, is the scrap brought so humorously to life by Hugh Grant and Colin Firth, in the film *Bridget Jones's Diary*. It is all most undignified!

If you are really stuck on how to begin, don't get hung up on trying to find the opening move. Start somewhere in the middle instead, give a few moves to the actors to see how they cope, and then develop the fight forwards and backwards from there. This way of

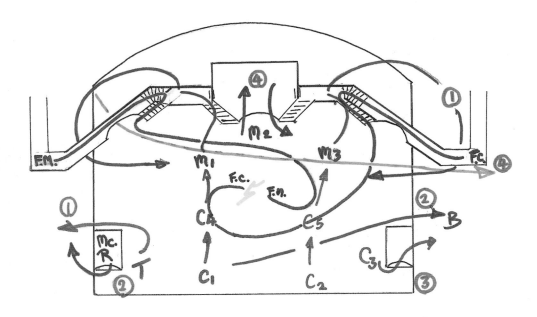

Fig 266 Flight paths: the opening rumble beween the Montagues and Capulets in Romeo og Julie, *choreographed for the Norwegian National Ballet.*

working does rely on having plenty of rehearsal time. If rehearsal time is limited, you need to have prepared the fight, or most of it, in advance. Remember, it is not how fast you

can work, teaching the actors the fight, but how long it takes them to learn, and to rehearse it up to a believable performance speed.

Floor patterns are very important – the more you vary the movements of the fight around the stage, using the set, the more interesting it is for the audience.

Early in my career, playing Laertes, I staged the fights for a repertory company's production of *Hamlet*. In my well-thumbed copy of William Hobbs' *Techniques of the Stage Fight*, I turned to the section on Movement. Inspired by the floor-pattern diagram and, remembering the words of Dame Edna Everage – 'Colour and movement, darlings! – I went to work planning my fight. A subsequent review said that my fight owed more to Hollywood than to Shakespeare. I was delighted.

WORKING WITH THE TEAM

As the fight director or arranger, you are not working in isolation. Theatre involves collaboration between the members of a creative team, and each person on that team will bring to the project their individual expertise. Communication is vital, as everyone has something to contribute.

The Director

The director is the one with the overall creative vision, so the fight arranger needs to get as much information as possible from him or her. Read the play before you meet them, remembering, however, that this guarantees only that you know the original story and that everything may change.

What does the director see as happening? What period are they setting the work in? Who are the actors involved and can they fight? Is it a duel between two people, or is it a battle? What is the budget for, and availability of, weapons?

The director may sit in while you rehearse and interject comments, or they may go away and come back to see how you are progressing. If the director sees work in progress remind them that it is just that – not the finished article. The actors need as much time as possible to rehearse and bring the fight up to performance speed.

Set Designer

The fight arranger needs to see a model of the set early on, or a least pictures of the scene in which he will be working. This will give rise to a number of questions.

How does the set affect the fight? Is the floor sloping (raked) and what is it made of? Where are the entrances and exits? What furniture is about? Can an actor swing on this, jump off that, fall against the other?

Costume Designer or Wardrobe

Are the clothes practical for the physical activity required? If your leading character is, for example, a swashbuckling hero – say, Zorro – his costume must allow for plenty of movement! He must have trousers that stretch when he lunges or leaps off his fibreglass stallion. Jackets and shirts must allow him to raise his arms above his head and move flamboyantly, and everything must be made in materials that breathe and can be washed frequently.

The character may need protective pads for his back, elbows or knees, to be sewn into his costume, or worn under it for that roll down the stairs (as in Michael Frayn's play *Noises Off*).

Shoes and boots need to fit well and have non-slip soles, and the actor will need to have them as soon as possible in rehearsals.

Will the wardrobe be supplying the dress-swords and accoutrements – belts, frogs and baldricks (*see* Fig 267) – or does everything need to be hired from an armourer.

> Working for the Danish Royal Ballet on a production of Kermessen i Brügge, I was checking up on the swords needed and discovered that there was no armoury – rather, it was split between the costume department and the props department. The swords that the actors wore on to the stage were the responsibility of the costume department but the swords that were handed to the actor on stage came from Props!
>
> A division of labour, too far, perhaps.

Props

The fight arranger will need to liaise with the props department if there is anything on the set that he wishes to incorporate in the fight, or if he wants any special makes, for example, break-away furniture.

L.X. (Lighting)

Special effects such as flashes, strobe lights or smoke will be discussed during rehearsals, but you will not see the lighting state for the fight until the technical or dress rehearsal. Check that the actors can see each other and the weapons they are using! Check too, that they are not blinded by any lanterns (hung low or set in the wings).

Fig 267 In red, a plain belt with attached frog for a broadsword or a rapier; in green, a broadsword frog; to the left, in black, a military-style belt with clips for the scabbard; in the centre, in black and silver, an Elizabethan rapier belt with frog; in fur, a loop of leather for a latex LARP sword; in brown, a baldrick.

Sound

Is there music (recorded or live) under-scoring your fights? Do you need special effects for a battle, a neck-break, a slap – a drummer in the pit for pantomime effects such as a kick to the unmentionables, a frying pan in the face, a 'slosh' scene?

Soundtracks

Audiences have become so used to the musical soundtrack in films that sometimes they are not aware of it. But they can be very aware of a lack of sound in the theatre. Why not accompany your stage fight with music?

Imagine how much fun I had creating a swashbuckling pirate battle to the number *El*

Bravo!, for the British production of Barry Manilow's *Copacabana*.

Soundscape

One alternative to music is to create your own soundscape.

In a very effective battle scene in *St Joan* at London's National Theatre in 2007, a vibrant and intense atmosphere was created by the use of a certain style of performance, made famous by *Stomp*.

In another production, a Shakespeare play, the sword-fights were done without swords (due to the close proximity of the audience). The musical director used a synthesizer to create all the sounds of the fight, such as the drawing of the sword, the swishes, and the clash and clamour of steel on steel.

Stage Management

These are very important people, particularly whoever is 'on the book' (the prompt copy). They run the show. If you make a fight script (*see* 'Notation'), give them a copy for the book, and get them to video the fight as well. The stage-management team will also be responsible for the maintenance of the weapons. If they do not know how to do this, take them through what you require (*see* page 181).

The Actors

Quite simply, the job of the fight arranger is to make the actors look good, fighting, as it were, to the manner born. They may not be particularly physical, or have the time, inclination or patience to practise the techniques, but you have a job to do as well. Keep the fight simple, tell the story and suit the action to the word.

Take as an example the fight between Mercutio and Tybalt in *Romeo and Juliet* . It can be a show-piece for actors who can fight (and a nightmare for those who cannot). Shakespeare's stage direction is simply 'They fight', but Benvolio's description, beginning 'With piercing steel at bold Mercutio's breast' (Act III, Scene ii), mentions only four attacks with the swords (and two hand parries). The fourth is the envious thrust that mortally wounds Mercutio.

When planning a fight, start move by move. Create phrases of one or three or five moves. A fight can be just one move, if that one move is exactly what is required. After just a few phrases, you could be done. The fight does not need to have dozens of moves to be brilliant.

The next stage is to build the fight, slowly and patiently, making sure that the actors know what they are doing and why. Alter moves if they do not work, or if the actor can-

not do them, or (more usually) if they claim that their character would never do that.

Throw in a couple of curves – moves that the audience are not expecting. Just because one character wins, he does not have to have the upper hand throughout the entire fight. The fight is in sections, so it is reasonable to assume that he may lose a couple of rounds at some point.

NOTATION

You will be writing down your fight for yourself, as you create it, so give a copy to the deputy stage manager on the book. This will be a record to which the actors will be able to refer when rehearsing, if you are not around. Should the show run for a long time and be re-cast, the new cast will of course need rehearsing. Alternatively, the show may come to an end, but be revived later (as sometimes happen with opera and ballet). Both situations will need an accurate record. In addition, should there be an accident in a fight performance, there is a record of the moves that were actually set and how it should have been safely performed.

Video is the simplest method of notating and these days you do not even need a camera! Anyone with a modern mobile phone can now make a record of a fight, as each section is finished.

Notating a fight in writing can be done in several ways, but in any case you need to make sure that the stage management and the actors can not only read it, but also understand it. Too often, fight directors develop their own unintelligible shorthand. My own notes make perfect sense in the moment, but a year or two later even I have trouble interpreting them!

The Long-Hand Method

The fight is recorded in the same way as an author describing action in a book:

Fig 268 The Nutcracker *score.*

'A enters the room, brandishing his sword and, seeing B about to escape out of the window, attacks with a mighty cut to his waist. B just manages to block A's attack and, twirling his sword around his head, responds in similar fashion. A, advancing, contemptuously knocks this aside and, raising his sword, beats down upon the head of the unfortunate B, who just manages to raise his sword in time, but the force of the blow knocks him clean out of the window.'

The A and B Methods
'A: attacks with bish – parries 4 – finishes with a bosh.

B: defends by parrying 2 – attacks with a bash – parrys 5 – falls out of the window.'

Or:

'A: attacks with a bish; B defends with a parry 2.

A: parries with a 4; B responds with a bash.

A: continues with a bosh; B just manages to parry his head (5) but falls out of the window!'

Notating on a Musical Score
Where music is involved, as in a musical, ballet or opera, the person creating the fight listens over and over to the music and then writes in the score what should happen.

The score of Tchaikovsky's ballet *The Nutcracker* (*see* Fig 268) shows the moment of the arrival of the mice and toy soldiers, just before the battle begins. One-third of the way through the battle, the Mouse Sergeant is trapped by the Cavalry, while the foot-soldiers line up ready to march down on the unprotected mice. The choreography is a tribute to Sergei Eisenstein's 1925 film *Battleship Potemkin*, and the iconic scene in which troops march down the Odessa Steps, firing on the

Fig 269 Battle from **The Nutcracker.**

173

Fig 270 The battle continues.

Fig 271 The Nutcracker defeats the Mouse King.

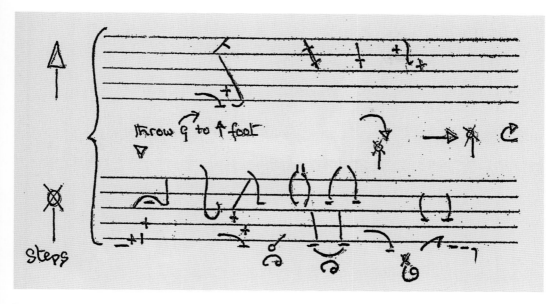

Fig 272 Benesh notation Romeo and Juliet – a rehearsal copy of the moment when Mercutio challenges Tybalt to fight.

fleeing Russian civilians. A mother is shown at the top of the steps, while her baby in its pram bounces its way down the entire length of steps alongside the soldiers. The moment has been reproduced in many films, including the 1987 film *The Untouchables*, with Kevin Costner, Sean Connery and Andy Garcia.

Dance companies use two different forms of notation: Laban and Benesh. When I worked with Christopher Gable on Prokofiev's *Romeo and Juliet* with the Northern Ballet Theatre, the production was notated in the Benesh system by someone specifically trained to write, and read it. The system uses symbols that represent the various positions and movements of the body, which are drawn on to a five-line stave, similar to that used in a musical score (Fig 272).

It is very difficult to describe in words, or in any form of written notation, the sheer physical grace and power that a ballet dancer can bring to a fight; *see* instead the picture of Scott Casban as Tybalt in the Norwegian National Ballet's 2004 production of *Romeo og Julie* (Figs 273–275).

FIGHTS FOR PERFORMANCE

Performance Anxiety

The fight arranger needs to start to address any anxieties early on in rehearsals, by following certain guidelines:

* rehearse slowly and carefully, keeping the performance tempo as a final goal towards which everyone is working;
* before the performance, have a fight call (*see* page 177);
* backstage during performance, if the actors need a quick reminder, you can 'finger-

Fig 273 Tybalt makes his entrance in the Norwegian National Ballet's **Romeo og Julie.**

fight' the choreography as close as possible to going on.

On Stage

There are a number of issues for the fight arranger and the actors to consider when the actors are on stage:

* Eye contact must be made before starting the fight and before each separate sequence; it must also be re-established after turning your back – each partner is the other's life-line.

* The fight is not a race. There are no prizes for finishing first and, despite the story's outcome and who wins, the partners must finish together.

* At the beginning of the production's run, while the adrenaline is pumping hard, it is important to keep the start of the fight under control. If the performers begin by giving 100 per cent, not only will they have nowhere to go, they will physically and emotionally run out of steam and the fight will end not with a bang but with a whimper.

* By the second week, the adrenaline and performance nerves will be under control and the fight will be looking good, beautifully danced.
* Some people believe that fighting harder and faster, and being closer to their partner is more exciting. To whom? Certainly not to the partner. When actors are excited while performing, they are not necessarily exciting to watch.
* Do not hold your breath during the fight; remember to breathe out!
* Do not worry about remembering the moves. Like dialogue, you only need to remember the opening and the rest will flood back.
* In case anything goes wrong – a move forgotten, a broken weapon – both partners should step back. There should be a pre-arranged visual or verbal cue to re-start the fight, and this must be practised in rehearsals. You can go back to the beginning of the phrase or go on to the next one. However, if you or your partner has completely lost the plot, die off stage!
* There is no room for invention or improvisation of fight moves in a performance.
* In battles or group fights, everyone needs to be aware of everyone else around them. Stick to your fighting area and flight path and most importantly, do not alter the rhythm or tempo of your fight, which is just one part of the choreographed whole.
* Finally, observe the sage advice given by American fight master Alan Suddeth, in his excellent book *Fight Directing for the Theater*, and be the best partner you can be!

Warm-Up

Always have a warm-up before the fight call. Not only will it prepare the actors for the performance and its physical requirements, but it is also excellent for sloughing off the cares of the outside world that they have just left. At the same time, it will help everyone to focus on the job in hand and on the people with whom they are about to work.

Fight Calls

No matter how small the fight is, a fight call should be held prior to the first performance of each day, in the performance space. This should be a run-through of the fight as it happens in performance – first at a relaxed tempo, as a mental and physical reminder, and then at performance speed. It should be supervised by a fight captain, if there is one, or equivalent. It is usually done half an hour before the half-hour call, giving the actors time to get into make-up and allowing the stage management to re-set the stage, weapons and props.

Fight Captains

'Fight captain' is an American term, devised to complement the role of the 'dance captain' in the dance world. It is a person with fight experience who is there to keep an eye on the fight sequences in the show, if the fight arranger is not there to do it himself.

Substitute Weapons

It is always advisable to have one or two standby weapons on or near the stage in case of breakage during the show. They should, as far as possible, be the same type of weapon in terms of size, weight, and so on.

Weapons Backstage

Due care and attention should be taken at all times. Any person carrying a weapon backstage should be aware of where the point is at all times. It should not be over the shoulder, pointing forwards or backwards.

No one should run backstage with a weapon in their hands.

If a weapon has to be left on the side of the stage or in the wings, to be picked up later,

Fig 274 Tybalt attacks Mercutio.

or during a quick change, ensure that the weapon, particularly its point, cannot cause injury to anyone walking into it.

Alterations to the Fight

Ideally, the fight should be set, learnt and practised by the time it comes to the final runs in the rehearsal period. When the production moves from the rehearsal room into the performance space, the fight arranger or choreographer should be there to stage the fight, and deal with any problems that might arise.

After the first performance, the fight should not in any way be altered without proper rehearsal and, professionally speaking, the fight director's permission and subsequent attendance for the new rehearsals. An exception to this may arise in an emergency, when a dangerous move, or indeed the whole fight, may have to be cut completely.

Weapons in a Public Place

If you are required to handle weapons in a public space – for example, in a street performance, or a publicity event in the street or a shopping centre – you must notify the local police (having familiarized yourself with any new laws) and any local security. You do not want to be arrested for carrying offensive weapons or causing an affray.

The performance must be confined to a defined area, with a barrier cordoning the public off.

If you are taking part in an event such as a medieval fair, a carnival parade or joust, check with the event organizers about the wearing and use of weapons.

When weapons are being transported (to and from a venue, from the armourer, and so on), by hand, they must carried in a bag, such as a fencing bag designed to carry swords. If you are transporting them by car, put them in a bag or box, and in the boot. It should not be obvious to the general public that you are carrying a weapon and, of course, even if you get into a spot of bother, it should never be taken out and used defensively.

Identification

It is very important that you always carry documents from your theatre, company or school giving you the authority to be in possession of the weapons on their behalf, together with the reasons why you are carrying them.

If they are weapons that need a licence (deactivated guns), make sure you carry that documentation too.

Fig 275 The death of Tybalt.

HEALTH AND SAFETY

Risk Assessment

Safety is basic common sense, once you know what to look out for. The HSE guidance document *Five Steps to Risk Assessment* recommends three steps in the first instance:

1. look for the hazards;
2. decide who might be harmed and how;
3. evaluate the risks and decide whether the existing precautions are adequate or whether more should be done.

Hamlet's words are always relevant, when he says, 'If it be now, tis not to come; if it be not to come, it will be now; if it be not now, yet it will come: the readiness is all...' (*Hamlet* Act V, Scene ii).

Basically, accidents do happen. If they have not yet, they will some time. Until then, it is important to do everything practically possible to prevent them, and to be ready to react to any situation in a positive manner.

Past or Current Injuries and Other Risks

Check over the people who are fighting. Have they had any injuries that might affect them during rehearsal and performance, or might become worse while stage fighting? In addition, anyone who is hungover, or who has been drinking or taking drugs, must not be permitted to rehearse, practise or perform stage fighting.

They must have appropriate work clothes, good shoes, and pads for knees and backs if necessary.

The space where the actors are working must have a clean, dry floor, with no uneven surfaces, and no trip hazards. The temperature, ventilation and lighting must be adequate, and the room must be big enough for the number of people who are working in it and/or for the weapons being used. This includes a sufficiently high ceiling with no lights dangling low.

The condition of all weapons, props and any piece of furniture, scenery or set that you might be using must be checked.

When working, the fight arranger needs to make sure that all performers warm up and down, take regular water breaks, and are careful not to attempt techniques beyond their physical capabilities. No one should push themselves to exhaustion.

First Aid

First aid can help only in the immediate aftermath of a problem and, if there is any doubt, medical advice must be sought.

Make sure that you have an up-to-date first aid kit, with hypoallergenic plasters, and that there is a qualified first-aid person available during training. When working in hired prem-

---

PRICE

P: PROTECTION. The injured part of the body should be protected against further injury or strain (for example, by using crutches).

R: REST. Rest the injured part of the body as much as possible for about two days.

I: ICE. Ice the injured area with crushed ice, ice-pack, ice-cubes, a pack of frozen peas, running cold water or the equivalent. NB: ice should not be put directly on to the skin. Icing must be repeated evenly: 20 minutes every 2 hours for the first 24 hours (the acute phase) after the injury.

C: COMPRESSION. Wrap an elastic bandage around the injured area, both under and over the ice-pack. The bandage must not be so tight that the skin becomes blue.

E: ELEVATION. The injured part of the body should be elevated while resting. This reduces the blood pressure in the area and reduces the bleeding.

---

ises, check their Health and Safety Regulations and Procedures. Make sure someone has a mobile phone, should you need to call for help.

Practical Procedures
in Case of Injury

The following practical instructions are given to the professional dancers in the Norwegian National Ballet, Oslo:

1. One or two people should take responsibility for ensuring quiet and calm around the injured person.
2. Check whether the injured person can move or put weight on the injured part of the body.
3. If they can, they should follow the PRICE principle; go home and continue with PRICE for the next 24 hours; if there is no improvement after that, seek medical advice.
4. If they cannot put weight on the injured part, or if there is a sudden swelling, or blue/red and warm skin around the injury, follow the PRICE principle as far as practically possible; go to the local hospital casualty department and seek professional aid; call an ambulance.

PREPARATION AND
STORAGE OF WEAPONS
FOR THE STAGE

If the weapons are to be used for fighting, as opposed to being decorative, they should be theatrical or re-enactment versions, which are made to take a constant bashing. Real or antique weapons will not be up to the job.

All edged and pointed weapons used for rehearsal and in performance should be blunt unless the action of the play specifically requires otherwise (for example, if they are to be used to slice food). If a cutting weapon is required in the fight, a blunt duplicate should be substituted as soon as possible.

For rehearsal and performance, make a sword-rack or a box, rather than leaving weapons lying around on the floor where they can be trodden on or have another prop or piece of furniture dumped upon them. Bends and kinks will eventually lead to snapping, so weapons need a dedicated space. Overnight, keep them out of sight in a locked room. A shiny sword is a very tempting target to a passing human jackdaw.

If the weapons have been in cold storage, even if only overnight, they should be placed somewhere warm to prevent the brittle blades from snapping. Northern Ballet Theatre has a special box with a heating element inside to keep blades at room temperature.

On tour, a secure box is ideal to keep all weapons safely together, and to protect them from mishandling.

MAINTENANCE OF
EDGED WEAPONS

The amount of maintenance you do will depend on two things: the quality of the weapons you are using, and the amount of blade-to-blade contact in the fight.

Swords

Some maintenance will usually have to be done daily between shows.

Loose Handles

The technique for tightening loose handles is quite simple. Through the handle of the sword passes the tang (Fig 276). For fighting swords, it should be a continuation of the blade, not just an extra bit soldered on. It will have a threaded end on which the pommel is mounted. The pommel will either screw on itself or slide on and then be held in place by a locking nut.

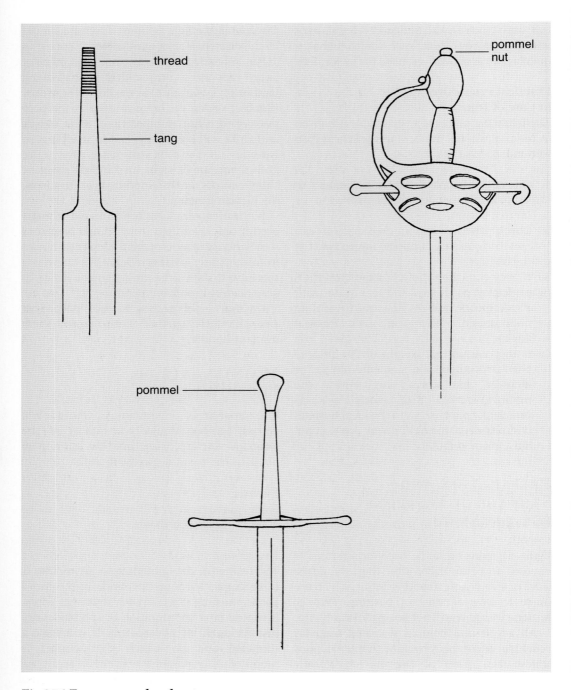

Fig 276 Tang, pommel and nut.

To tighten, twist the pommel until the sword is secure and the blade 'tings'. This can even be done by the actor during the fight if necessary. To tighten it using the locking nut, hold the blade firmly with a pair of pliers, as close to the grip as possible, and tighten until it gives a satisfying 'ting'.

Note: be careful not to over-tighten, as this may either strip the thread on the tang (particularly if it made of aluminium) or stress the point at which the shoulders of the blade meet the tang, which may then break.

Serrated Edges

During the fight, notches and splinters will be caused by the blades clashing, edge against edge, whether the sword is made from steel, aluminium or wood.

Splinters on the blade of a sword will tear any skin with which it comes into contact, as well as the fabric of costumes. To prevent this, remove splinters from the sword edge by placing the weapon in a vice, and smoothing away the damage with a file. Be sure to work both angles, finally running the file down the centre of the edge to make sure you have not sharpened it! Using an electric grinder will be easier and faster, but it is not recommended, as any undue pressure can take off more than the intended amount, leaving the blade seriously grooved and potentially weakened.

As a final check, lightly run a cloth down the length of the cutting edge. If the blade is smooth, the cloth should not snag on the blade.

Rust

To remove surface rust from a steel weapon, try using a flexible sander (sandpaper wrapped around a flexible sponge). The sander can be obtained in various strengths. You could also use an emery paper or cloth with a light coating of 3-in-1 oil. Try to avoid scratching the steel.

Cracking and Fatigue

All blades, after prolonged use or misuse, can develop cracks and snap without warning. Detection of this is particularly difficult, as the blade may look fine to the naked eye. However, there is an audible indication of something wrong when, having tightened the sword, the blade does not 'ting', giving instead a dull sound.

X-raying the blade is the only sure way to detect cracks and the Norwegian National Ballet does exactly that. Their ballets are seasonal, the swords may often be stored away for a long period of time, without use, and they take their safety very seriously indeed.

Changing a Blade

This is relatively easy, particularly if you are using, for example, a sport epée blade. It is always best, however, to have a complete spare weapon to hand and then you can just return the broken parts to the armourer.

Refurbishing

When the show is over and hired weapons are to be returned, it is always good practice to smooth down and clean them first. If you are keeping them you will do this anyway in preparation for any long-term storage. An armourer might, for a fee, agree to refurbish the weapons for you.

Knives

The same care should be applied to knives as to swords, although they may not need the same amount of daily attention. Blood-letting knives usually have a rubber bulb in the handle or pommel, which, when squeezed, forces the blood through a tube in the hollow blade to exit through a small hole either in the cutting edge or at the point. Care must be taken in washing out the blood thoroughly.

The edge or point, which may make contact with the victim, should be frequently checked to see that it remains completely smooth.

Retractable blades need particular care. These weapons work on the principle of a spring concealed in the handle. It is important to see that both the spring and the blade are kept lightly oiled for the action to function smoothly.

Cosmetic blood, which is used in conjunction with these knives, could, if left to congeal, cause the blade to stick at the vital moment, preventing it from completely retracting.

Large-Edged Weapons

While the blades of polearms, axes, spears, and so on, rarely come into contact with fighting swords, particular care should be paid to the point where the head of the weapon is attached to the pole or shaft. The pole or shaft is usually made from wood and can be used in a fight, like a quarterstaff, making contact with blades. Check for short-term damage, splinters and, long term, cracks in the wood.

Shields

Check the handles and/or straps that are used to hold the shield, as well as the edges of the shield, which can easily splinter or crack. Make sure that the front is not rusty or too dented from severe bashing. If the shield has decorative nails, check that they are still there and not scattered around on the stage – usually pin-end up!

LONG-TERM STORAGE

All weapons should first be cleaned and the metal ones lightly oiled or greased to prevent rusting. They should then, if at all possible, be stored in racks made for the purpose – scabbards separately – and not laid down somewhere or simply piled into a cupboard.

BIBLIOGRAPHY

Books on Stage Fighting

From the UK

Brown, Terry, *English Martial Arts* (Anglo-Saxon Books, 1997)

Gordon, Gilbert, *Stage Fights: A Simple Handbook of Techniques* (J. Garnet Miller Ltd, 1973)

Hobbs, William, *Fight Direction for Stage and Screen* (A. & C. Black, London, 1995)

Hobbs, William, *Techniques of the Stage Fight* (Studio Vista Ltd, 1967)

Hobbs, W., *Stage Combat* (Barrie & Jenkins, London, 1980)

Marshall, Henry, *So You Want to be Errol Flynn* (Marymount College, 1977)

Wise, A., *The History and Art of Personal Combat* (Hugh Evelyn, 1971)

Wise, A., *Weapons in the Theatre* (Longman, 1968)

From the USA

Boughn, Jenn Zuko, *Stage Combat: Fisticuffs, Stunts and Swordplay for Theater and Film* (Allworth Press, New York, 2006)

Girard, Dale Anthony, *The Fight Arranger's Companion* (privately published, Second Edition, 1995–96)

Girard, Dale Anthony, *Actors on Guard* (Routledge, New York & London, 1997)

Katz, Albert M., *Stage Violence: The Theatre Student Series* (Richards Rosen Press Inc., NY, 1976)

Kezer, Claude D., *Principles of Stage Combat Handbook* (Players Press Inc., Studio City, CA, 1995)

Kirkland, Michael, Stage Combat Resource Materials

Lane, R., *Swashbuckling: A step-by-step guide to the art of stage combat and theatrical swordplay* (Nick Hern Books, London, 1999)

Martinez, J.D., *Combat Mime: A Non-Violent Approach to Stage Violence* (Nelson-Hall Publishers, Chicago, 1982)

Strider, J.D., *Techniques for Training for Stage Fighting* (Studies in Theatre Arts, June 1999 College Level)

Suddeth, J. Allen., *Fight Directing for the Theatre* (Heinemann, Portsmouth, NH, 1996)

From New Zealand

Wolf, Tony (ed.) *The Bartitsu Compendium* (www.lulu.com ID: 138834)

Other Related Books

Arbeau, Thoinot, *Orchesography* (Dover Publications Inc., NY, 1967)

Aylward, J.D., *The English Master of Arms* (Routledge & Kegan Paul, 1956)

Aylward, J.D., *The Small-Sword in England* (Hutchinson's Scientific & Technical Publications, c. 1945)

The Badminton Library of Sports and Pastimes: Fencing, Boxing, Wrestling (Spottiswoode and Co., London, 1890)

Bell and Daldy, *The Works of Tacitus* (Oxford Translation, London, 1871)

Flynn, Errol, *My Wicked, Wicked Ways* (Mandarin Paperbacks, 1992)

Haddon, Celia, *The First Ever English Olimpick Games* (Hodder & Stoughton, 2004)

BIBLIOGRAPHY

Hutton, Alfred, *Old Sword Play* (Dover Publications Inc., NY 2001)

Hutton, Alfred, *Cold Steel* (Dover Publications Inc., NY, 2006)

Lee, Bruce, *Tao of Jeet Kune Do* (O'hara Publications Inc., California, 1975, Library of Congress: 75-24803)

Morton, E.D., *Martini A–Z of Fencing* (Macdonald Queen Anne Press, ISBN 0-356-154394)

Oakeshott, R. Ewart., *A Knight and his Weapons* (Tutterworth Press, 1964)

Oakeshott, R. Ewart., *The Sword in the Age of Chivalry* (Arms and Armour Press, London, 1981)

Pitman, Brian, *Fencing: Techniques of Foil, Epée and Sabre* (The Crowood Press, 2005)

R-C Annie, via the BADC website, 'Risk Assessment for Stage and Screen Combat'

Rector, Mark, *Medieval Combat* (Hans Talhoffer Greenhill Books, London 2006)

Richards, Jeffrey, *Swordmen of the Screen* (Routledge & Kegan Paul Ltd., 1977, IBSN 0 7100 8478 1)

Schulze, Carl and Verhulsdonk, Torsten, *Talhoffer's Fechtbuch* (Vs-Books, 1998, ISBN 3-932077-03-2)

Tegner, Bruce, *Aikido and Holds and Locks* (Corgi Books, 1971)

Tegner, Bruce, *Stick Fighting for Self-Defense* (Thor Publishing Co., LA, 1961)

Westbrook, A. and Ratti, O., *Aikido and the Dynamic Sphere* (Charles E. Tuttle Company, Rutland, Vermont and Tokyo, Japan, 1970)

FILMOGRAPHY

GREEK AND ROMAN

Demetrius and the Gladiators (Twentieth Century Fox 1954; Victor Mature)

Gladiator – Sword (Universal and Dreamworks Pictures 2000; Russell Crowe; Stunt Co-ordinator Nick Powell)

Spartacus – Sword (Universal Pictures 1960. Kirk Douglas)

Troy – Spear and shield (Warner Bros. 2004; Brad Pitt and Eric Bana; Swordmaster Richard Ryan and Stunt Co-ordinator Simon Crane)

BROADSWORD

The Adventures of Robin Hood (Warner Bros. 1938; Errol Flynn and Basil Rathbone; Swordmaster Fred Cavens).

Highlander (Warner Bros. 1989; Christopher Lambert; Swordmaster Bob Anderson and Peter Diamond)

Monty Python and the Holy Grail: (National Film Trustee Co. 1974; Graham Chapman and John Cleese; Swordmaster John Waller)

SINGLE RAPIER

D'Artagnan's Daughter (Artificial Eye Video 1994; Sophie Marceau; Swordmasters Claude & Michel Carliez)

Shakespeare in Love (Miramax and Universal Studios 1998; Swordmaster William Hobbs)

The Princess Bride (1987; Swordmaster Bob Anderson & Stunt Co-ordinator Peter Diamond)

The Three Musketeers (MGM 1948; Gene Kelly; Swordmaster Jean Heremans)

RAPIER AND DAGGER

Anne of the Indies (R.K.O.1951; Jean Peters; Swordmaster Fred Cavens)

Don Juan (1948; Errol Flynn and Robert Douglas; Swordmaster Fred Cavens)

Hamlet (Laurence Olivier and Terence Young; Swordmaster Patrick Crean)

SMALLSWORD

Le Bossu (1999; Daniel Auteuil, Marie Gillain and Vincent Perez; Swordmasters Claude and Michel Carliez)

The Duellist (Paramount Pictures 1977; Keith Carradine and Harvey Keital; Swordmaster William Hobbs)

Scaramouche (MGM 1952; Stewart Granger and Mel Ferrer; Swordmaster Jean Heremans)

FENCING SWORDS

By the Sword (The Movie Group 1991; Eric Roberts and F. Murray Abraham; Swordmaster Bob Anderson)

The Great Race (1965; Tony Curtis, Natalie Wood and Ross Martin)

SABRE

The Duellist (*see* Smallsword)

The Prisoner of Zenda (1937; Ronald Coleman and Douglas Fairbanks Jnr.; Swordmaster Ralph Faulkner)

The Mark of Zorro (Tristar Pictures 1998; Anthony Hopkins, Antonio Banderas and Catherine Zeta-Jones; Swordmaster Bob Anderson)

MIXED AND OTHER

Enter the Dragon – Staff, Sticks, Nunchaku – (Warner Bros. 1973; *Bruce* Lee)

Kill Bill Vol 1 – Samurai Sword and Ball & Chain – (Miramax Films; Uma Thurman and Chiaki Kuriyama)

The Mummy Returns – Sai – (Universal Studios 2001; Rachel Weisz and Patricia Velasquez)

Rob Roy – Transitional Rapier and Highland Broadsword – (United Artists Pictures 1995; Liam Neeson and Tim Roth; Swordmaster William Hobbs)

The Seven Samurai, Sanjuro, Throne of Blood, Yojimbo (Akira Kurosawa and Toshiro Mifune)

CHINESE SWORDS

Crouching Tiger, Hidden Dragon (Colombia Pictures Film Production Asia 2000; Chow Yun Fat, Michelle Yeoh and Zhang Zi Yi)

Hero (Miramax 2002; Jet Li, Zhang Zi Yi)

House of Flying Daggers (Elite Group Enterprises Inc. 2003; Zhang Zi Yi)

KNIFE

Blood Wedding (First Class Films 1983; Antonio Gades)

The Hunted (Lakeshore Entertainment and Paramount 2002; Tommy Lee Jones)

West Side Story (Mirisch Pictures 1961; Russ Tamblyn and George Chakiris; choreography Jerome Robbins)

Under Siege 1 & 2 (Warner Bros. 1992/5; Steven Seagal)

QUARTERSTAFF

Robin Hood (with Alan Hale; *see* Broadsword)

Star Wars 1 – The Phantom Menace (Lucas Film Ltd. 2000; Liam Neeson, Ewan McGregor and Ray Park)

UNARMED COMBAT

Any *Bruce Lee, Jackie Chan, Jet Li* Film

The Bourne Identity (Universal 1998; Matt Damon; Stunt Co-ordinator Nick Powell)

Charlie's Angels (Columbia 2000/2003; Cameron Diaz, Drew Barrymore and Lucy Liu)

The Matrix (Village Roadshow Films 1999; Keanu Reeves, Laurence Fishburne, Carrie-Anne Moss and Hugo Weaving)

The Quiet Man (Republic Entertainment Inc., 1952; John Wayne)

The Transporter (Twentieth Century Fox 2002; Jason Statham)

GUNS

Equilibrium (Miramax and Dimension Films 2002; Christian Bale)

Tomb Raider (Paramount Pictures 2001/2003; Angelina Jolie)

Underworld (Screen Gems and Lakeshore Entertainment 2003; Kate Beckinsale)

TEACHING VIDEOS AND DVDs

Anthony de Longis: *Broadsword for the Stage and Screen* (2001) and *Rapier for the Stage and Screen* (1991) www.delongis.com/PalpableHit/

Ramon Martinez: *La Verdadera Destreza – The True Art and Skill of Spanish Swordmanship* (2002) www.delongis.com/PalpableHit/

Mike Loades: *The Blow by Blow Guide to Swordfighting in the Renaissance Style* (1992, Running Wolf Productions)

F. Braun McAsh: *The Practice of Arms – Beginning Swordwork for Stage and Film* (Cord Productions Ltd.) www.swordandstage.com

Royal Armouries (Leeds): *Masters of Defence* (1990)

Graziano Galvani: *Nova Scrimia* (Budo International Publishing Co.)

Alan Suddeth and David Leong: Unarmed Combat Videos 1 – 2 – 3.

Learning the Basics; Perfecting the Fundamentals; Mastering the Techniques (Combat Masters International)

APPENDIX – MOVEMENT DIAGRAMS

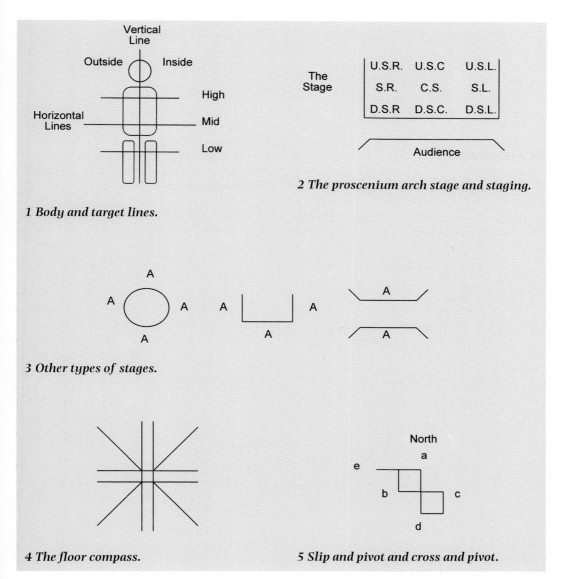

1 Body and target lines.

2 The proscenium arch stage and staging.

3 Other types of stages.

4 The floor compass.

5 Slip and pivot and cross and pivot.

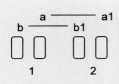

6 The side-step.

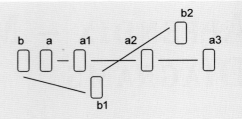

7 The crossing step.

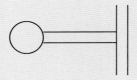

8 A stepping exercise.

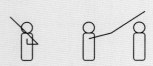

9 Vertical cut to the head.

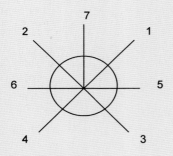

10 The wheel-cut diagram.

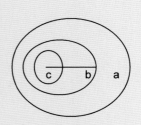

11 Safety in distance.

12 Parrying outside the body.

INDEX

INDEX